Love
EMBROIDERY

Love Embroidery is an original work, first published in 2012 in the United Kingdom by Future Publishing Limited in magazine form under the title *Love Embroidery*. This title is printed and distributed in North America under license. All rights reserved.

ISBN 978-1-57421-612-7

© 2013 by Design Originals, www.d-originals.com, an imprint of Fox Chapel Publishing, 800-457-9112, 1970 Broad Street, East Petersburg, PA 17520.

Printed in China
First printing

Love EMBROIDERY

SIMPLE PROJECTS AND IDEAS FOR HAND AND MACHINE TECHNIQUES

EDITORS OF FUTURE PUBLISHING

Design Originals

an Imprint of Fox Chapel Publishing
www.d-originals.com

Love EMBROIDERY

95

46

101

74

84

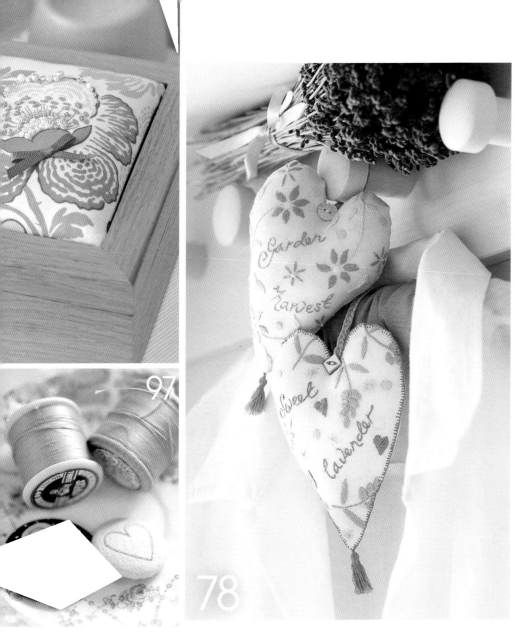

Exclusive!

9

designer
interviews

Aimee Ray Meet Aimee and
discover how she transforms
doodles into stitching

Welcome

to *Love* EMBROIDERY!

Inside you'll find an abundance of inspirational ideas, expert guidance and stunning projects, so you can fill your world with gorgeous embroidered items. Whether it's adorning fashion or items for your home, embroidery is the perfect way to get a personalized handmade look, quickly and easily – and embroidered goodies also make great gifts that your family and friends will adore.

Covering both hand embroidery, a traditional craft that's gained a fresh appeal, and freehand machine embroidery, a creative craft with a very modern style, you'll start with simple projects for both and move into more complex designs once you've mastered the basics.

Once you're comfortable with your stitching, try your hand on the beautiful baby suit on page 77, or on the pretty patchwork heart cushion on page 98. Or if you are feeling really creative, use your stitching knowledge and embroider a design of your own.

INTRODUCTION

The beautiful craft of embroidery covers a huge variety
of forms, styles and fashions, and its recent revival is
just one part of its long and fascinating history.

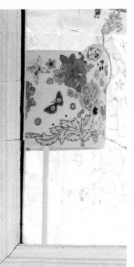

*This funky
lampshade by
Chloë Owens
is embellished
with machine
embroidery
and appliqué.*

The popularity of handmade fashion
and homewares is growing by leaps and
bounds – there's nothing so on-trend as
something you've made or embellished
yourself. Embroidery, in all its many
forms, is one of the easiest and most
beautiful ways to embellish your world,
so we're really excited to be able to use it
to personalize and create wonderful
projects that are also totally up-to-date.

Throughout the hundreds of years of
embroidery's history, there have been
many different types, stitches and styles
that have gone in and out of fashion.
From crewelwork in the Bayeux
Tapestry to wire-framed stumpwork,
right up to modern monochrome
blackwork, there's always been
something to suit all tastes. And it's no
different today – there's so much variety!

Love Embroidery focuses on freestyle
hand embroidery and machine
embroidery, as these are the easiest
styles to start with and are great for
creating fresh, modern designs. Before
we get started, though, let's take a quick
look at some of the different embroidery
styles you might have heard of…

This baby vest is hand embroidered with a cute strawberry motif – find out how on page 77.

Canvaswork is a densely stitched style of embroidery. These bright colors are worked in cushion, tent, mosaic and Gobelin filling stitches.

COUNTED CROSS STITCH

One of the most popular forms of embroidery, cross stitch is a great first technique to learn. It's also probably the oldest form of embroidery in the world. Cross stitch is a great way to create easy designs and patterns made of simple blocks, creating a decorative pattern over any evenweave fabric, where the warp and weft (vertical and horizontal) threads are the same size. Other stitches are also often used in cross stitch designs to add detail, such as backstitch and French knots.

FREESTYLE HAND EMBROIDERY

This technique is probably the most common type of embroidery you'll see. Unlike cross stitch, you don't have to follow the threads of the fabric – in this freestyle method, you can use almost any stitch in any way or direction you choose. Popular hand embroidery stitches include chain stitch, fly stitch, lazy daisies and French knots. Almost any kind of fabric and threads are suitable for this type of embroidery, although thinner fabrics may need backing for extra strength.

FREEHAND MACHINE EMBROIDERY

Your sewing machine is not restricted to stitching straight lines and corners. By adding a darning foot and lowering the feed dogs, you can stitch in any direction and create any shape, using a combination of straight stitch and zigzags. Altering your machine's tension can also bring the lower thread to the surface – try using a different bobbin color to the top stitch, which creates a pretty whip stitch.

Machine embroidery has been popular since the early 20th century, when Singer machines were used to recreate works of art, and techniques were developed to imitate traditional hand embroidery.

BEADED EMBROIDERY

Why not bling up your embroidery with a sparkling combination of seed beads, bugle beads, sequins, pearl beads and more? These beads are often used alongside other embroidery stitches and techniques, and are great for adding texture and sparkle to your work. Beaded embroidery is also perfect for creating glamorous accessories, such as purses or dress straps.

CREWELWORK

Made famous by the Bayeux Tapestry, crewelwork is simply freestyle hand embroidery created with wool threads, using a variety of stitches, and it's been popular since the Middle Ages. The stitches don't need to follow the weave of the fabric, which must be firm to support the weight of the dense stitches.

BLACKWORK

As its name implies, blackwork is a monochrome embroidery, which is usually worked in black on white or cream fabric, but it's also sometimes used with dark green, red or blue thread. It's a counted stitch embroidery, so you'll need to choose an evenweave fabric to work on, and most designs are worked in running stitch and double running stitch. A variety of stitch patterns are used to fill areas, and different numbers of threads are used to give varying thicknesses to the lines.

CANVASWORK (TAPESTRY)

One of the most flexible types of embroidery, canvaswork can be used to create anything from intricate pictures to glorious chair upholstery in country homes. Wool is most commonly used for the stitching and it was traditionally used to embellish furnishings and upholstery. This decorative embroidery is densely stitched onto a thick, even canvas until it completely covers the underlying fabric. Popular stitches include Gobelin stitch (satin stitch), cushion stitch, mosaic stitch, florentine stitch and tent stitch.

WHITEWORK

Clean and crisp, whitework is exactly what it sounds like – it can be done in various forms of embroidery, but always using white threads on white fabric, particularly cotton or muslin. The different stitches and threads create contrasting areas of light and shade, and it can involve pulled threadwork.

Whitework and blackwork create texture and shading through varied stitches in single colors.

CUTWORK

In cutwork, parts of the fabric are cut away to create holes once the embroidery is complete, creating an effect similar to lace. It's produced on fabric that doesn't fray easily, and the edges of the fabric are reinforced with a line of buttonhole stitches before cutting. The embroidery is usually worked in the same color thread as the fabric.

Hardanger is one of the most popular forms of cutwork. Delicate and pretty, Hardanger is a geometrically precise form of embroidery, which uses a variety of shapes such as squares, diamonds, stars and crosses. It was originally worked on white linen and in white or cream threads (so it is also part of the whitework family), but colored fabrics and threads are now also used.

GOLDWORK

Regarded throughout history as an indication of wealth and power, goldwork is still widely used in religious textiles and military regalia, and creates stunning pieces that are sure to draw attention. The term generally refers to any metallic threads, such as silver and copper, as well as real gold. These threads are held onto the fabric with tiny stitches, and a variety of stitches are used to reflect light in different ways, as well as using subtle pattern such as chevrons and bricking.

STUMPWORK

One of the most artistic forms of embroidery, stumpwork is like sculpture in embroidery. It originated in the 17th century, but was revived in the mid-20th century. The three-dimensional style uses padding or stuffing to raise specific shapes under the embroidery stitches of the background. Stumpwork is also often worked around a wire frame to create 3D objects, which are then fastened to the main fabric.

MY LIFE IN STITCHES…
Meet Embroidery Artist Aimee Ray

Aimee is an artist and embroiderer from the USA, who works on comic books and greetings cards, as well as hand embroidery. Her unique style of 'sketchy' stitching involves transferring a drawing onto fabric and embroidering freehand on top. She has an Etsy shop, www.etsy.com/shop/littledear, and her books, *Doodle Stitching* **and the sequel** *Doodle Stitching: The Motif Collection,* **are full of fun, quirky ideas.**

Q *You trained in graphic design. What first attracted you to working with textiles?*

A For as long as I can remember, I've loved making things out of paper, fabric, clay and whatever else I could get my hands on. I think I like textile work so much because it's so different from the computer design work I do all day. There's something primitive and relaxing about stitching by hand.

Q *There are many people who may not have tried your technique of embroidering freehand over a printed design before. Do you have any tips for them?*

A There are several ways to transfer a sketch to fabric. I normally trace it on using a light table (or a sunny window) and a fabric pen. As for freehand embroidery, you can start by learning one or two basic stitches, then just have fun. You can decide whether to follow the lines, or add details as the ideas come to you. I'm a 'make it up as I go along' person, so freehand embroidery is perfect for me.

Q *Why do you think the style of your designs is so popular?*

A My style is pretty loose, fanciful and whimsical. I like the idea that a drawing done in seconds can result in a detailed design.

Q *What one thing in your stash could you not live without?*

A I have lots of different colors of felt that I dip into for various projects. It's perfect for stuffed animals and it's easy to embroider on.

Q *What advice would you give to a first-time embroiderer?*

A Just relax and have fun. Embroidery doesn't need to be complicated – learn the basics and then use your imagination.

Q *What event in your life would you like to record in stitches?*

A All my work is a record of my life. Imagery from various places comes together in my subconscious and then spills out into my embroidery.

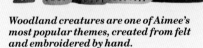

Aimee's set of five Russian Matryoshka dolls are really striking, with detailed embellishments.

Woodland creatures are one of Aimee's most popular themes, created from felt and embroidered by hand.

1 Prints charming

Get down to your local fabric shop and be inspired by all the gorgeous patterns and colors. Some fabrics feature motifs that are perfect for outlining or embellishing with hand embroidery, or using as appliqué motifs in a machine embroidery design. Look around and let the fabric inspire your next project.

10 *design* IDEAS

Now that you've got a taste for embroidery, find design inspiration with these top tips…

2 ETCH A SKETCH

You don't have to be great at art to draw your own designs. All you need is pencil and paper (and an eraser!) to draw simple shapes, such as flowers, stars and hearts, to then embroider. Even if your drawings aren't perfect, use modern fabrics and cheerful threads, and any quirky drawings will look great!

3 PRETTY PETALS

Try scanning real flowers into your computer – just be gentle with them, and clean your scanner glass afterwards. Print them out in color, then trace the outlines onto plain paper to create a pattern. Use the original colors of the petals to select the best threads and fabrics to use for a realistic look.

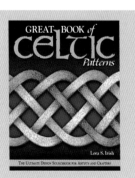

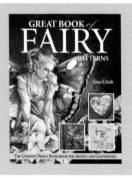

4 Page turners

Almost any outline can make an embroidery design, so you can find ideas in magazines, online (we love www.pinterest.com) and books.

5 Childhood charm

Get your little ones involved in embroidery by taking a drawing that your child or grandchild has done and turning it into an embroidered image for a T-shirt, book bag or special gift. Alternatively, how about embroidering their foot or hand print? Simply scan or photocopy it and then trace it with a washable fabric pen. Use satin stitch or a tight zigzag stitch on your machine to create thick, bold lines.

Drawing by Daniel Medus

Charlie aged 1

6 SAMPLING...

Samplers have been popular in embroidery since the 14th century, with a simple design and varied stitches. They often include the alphabet and numbers, and commemorate events such as weddings or births. Try stitching a few rows in different stitches or styles, then add the details of an event.

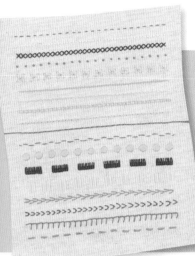

7 MAP HAPPY

Create a stitched map of somewhere meaningful to you – it could be the route you took on a special holiday, or a map of the important places in someone's life. The finished design can make a great gift. Try choosing a hand-dyed fabric in greens or blues for a true 'map' feel.

8 Through the lens

If you're not confident with drawing, try taking photos of items you'd like to embroider, or even scenery you'd like to capture. Print out the photos and then trace the key areas onto plain paper to create a pattern for hand embroidery, or appliqué and machine embroidery.

9 ON THE TILES

Tiled mosaic-style designs can look stunning in embroidery stitches. Keep an eye out for inspiration from flooring and architecture when you're on vacation, and be sure to take lots of pictures. Then draw or trace the outlines to create beautiful pieces. Strong and colorful geometric patterns will make for eye-catching designs.

10 Say it in stitches

Capture interesting sayings or phrases in embroidery. You can stitch lettering in various ways to create labels, or capture funny nicknames or amusing phrases that your children come up with. Or try 'subversive' embroidery, which is very popular – choose your favourite not-so-polite saying and decorate it with pretty flowers and cute animals, for a definite double-take when visitors see what you've created!

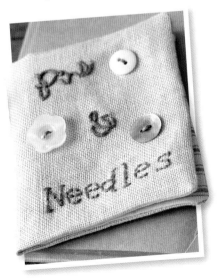

Hand embroidery basics

The art of creating beautiful
images in fabric and thread is
easy enough for anyone to do!
Your guide through
the basics…

Essential sewing supplies

If you're new to sewing, there are a few essential items you'll need to stock up on – assemble your supplies using our list below.

1 THREADS
There's a thread for almost every occasion and your local craft store can help you find the right one for your project. Many embroidery projects use embroidery floss, which is a great all-purpose thread. With embroidery floss, each thread length is made up of six strands of cotton twisted together. Most embroidery stitches are made using one or two strands of floss, but the project instructions should indicate how many strands to use when stitching different parts of your design. See page 16 for more details about threads.

2 BUTTONS
Buttons can be used for practical reasons, to secure the back of a cushion cover for instance, or just for decoration, to add texture and variety to your work.

3 FASTENINGS
Safety pins can hold fabrics together when ordinary pins may fall out. Snap fasteners and other fastenings, such as hooks and eyes, may also be useful.

4 SEAM RIPPER
If you're upcycling vintage fabrics or clothing, there are some occasions when you need this handy gadget to help your unpicking go smoothly and quickly.

5 THIMBLE
If you're regularly stitching or working with thicker fabrics, a thimble will save you from pricking your finger.

6 EMBROIDERY SCISSORS
At about 5in (13cm) long, these are much smaller than fabric scissors. The fine, straight blade makes them good for trimming stray threads.

7 NEEDLES
You can get specialist needles for embroidery and appliqué, but it's also handy to have a pack of assorted general-purpose sewing needles. For basic embroidery stitches, you'll need

an embroidery or crewel needle with a sharp tip, which is ideal for fine details such as backstitch and French knots.

8 THREAD CUTTER
These are great for when you're traveling or you don't have space for scissors. If you plan to take an embroidery project on a flight, check the airline's restrictions.

9 FABRIC
There's a huge range of different fabrics available, so your choice is almost limitless! Embroidery projects can be completed on almost any fabric, but always check the project instructions for

advice on which sort of fabric to use. If you're after a specific amount of fabric, you'll find it's usually sold by the yard or meter. However, some fabrics are sold in 'fat quarters', which are pieces measuring about 18x22in (45.5x56cm). See page 15 for more details about fabric.

10 PINS
Use these to hold pieces of fabric together. Regular dressmakers' pins can be tricky, so try pins with larger heads – these lie flat so you can iron over them.

11 FABRIC SCISSORS
Keep your fabric scissors sharp by only using them for fabric. Look for some

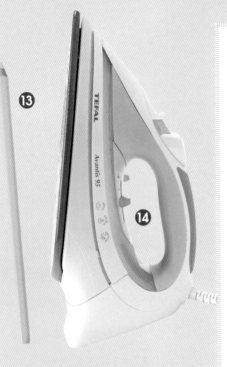

that are about 8in (20cm) long and have a curved handle to enable accurate cutting on flat surfaces, with pointed tips for precision.

12 TAPE MEASURE
Measuring your fabric correctly is one of the essential elements of creating a perfect embroidery design (measure twice, cut once!), so make sure you buy a tape measure that's at least 59in (150cm) long and has both metric and imperial units for quick conversions. Some have different colored sections to make measuring even easier.

13 FABRIC PENCIL
A fabric pencil is essential for tracing embroidery designs onto your fabric. They come in different shades, so you can find the color that stands out best on your material. You could also try a chalk pencil with a brush for erasing unwanted lines, or water-soluble pens and pencils that will disappear when you dampen or wash the fabric.

14 IRON
Crumpled fabrics can cause stitching mishaps, so you'll usually need to press your material before you start stitching. An iron is also useful for attaching appliqué shapes using fusible webbing. Use an ironing cloth or a tea towel to protect delicate fabrics when you iron them, and only iron on the reverse side.

Hoops & frames
Although not absolutely essential, we do recommend using an embroidery hoop or frame to keep an even stitching tension.

Seat frame
This sort of frame is an ingenious tool for embroidery! The frame consists of a wooden hoop, plus stand and wooden base, which you sit on to hold in place. It's the best option for anyone who prefers stitching with both hands.

Plastic clip frame
A simple clip frame is a great interlocking option. The hollow plastic tubes make the frame super-light – ideal for stitching on the move. Simply place your stitching over the frame and use the plastic clips to secure in place.

Interlocking bar frame
With this sort of versatile frame, you can create the perfect size every time by mixing and matching the wooden lengths. Stretch your fabric over the frame and secure using pins.

Wooden hoop
A simple wooden hoop is by far the most economical option, with various sizes available and most costing just a few dollars. Just be sure not to place your hoop over previously stitched work.

All about fabric

There are hundreds of fabrics out there, so we'll help you understand your options and pick the perfect material for every project.

WOVEN FABRICS ❶

Take a close look at a woven fabric and you'll see that it's made from two groups of threads, a warp (the threads that run lengthwise) and a weft (the threads that run widthwise). It will also have a border called a selvage, which is more tightly woven to prevent the fabric from unraveling (don't use this in your stitching). Cotton is one of the world's most popular woven fabrics. It's strong, easy to work with and can be washed at high temperatures. However, it wrinkles easily, so it's often blended with other fibers. Linen, woven from flax fibers, is even stronger than cotton, although it also has a tendency to crease.

NON-WOVEN FABRICS ❷

Unlike the straight warp and weft of woven materials, knitted fabrics use loops of yarn running in rows or columns. These fabrics are much more flexible and stretchy than woven cloth. You can easily embroider onto these fabrics but be aware that the area you stitch onto won't stretch as much afterwards. It's also essential to use a hoop on stretchy fabrics, for an even tension. Many non-woven fabrics are created by compressing individual fibers into a solid mass. One example of this is interfacing, which is a type of fabric that provides an extra layer of support to your material and stiffens it. Choose an interfacing that's slightly lighter than your fabric, and if you're using a fusible (iron-on) option then always test it on a scrap of the fabric. Make sure you attach it to the fabric before adding your embroidery.

FELT, NET AND LACE ❸

Felt is created by condensing woolen fibers, either using a machine or by hand in soapy water. You can also felt knitted fabric by putting it in a washing machine at a high temperature. This fabric is particularly popular with crafters and embroidery beginners because it's fray-resistant, doesn't stretch like woven materials and can easily be cut to any shape. Net and lace are fabrics created without compressing, weaving or knitting – both of these are made by knotting together lengths of thread to create a pattern. These materials are often used as decoration, and are best cut with small, sharp scissors for a neat finish. Always check what your fabric is made from before you wash it, in case of shrinkage.

GO SHOPPING

Collecting fabrics for your stash is fun, but if you have a particular project in mind, then it's best not to impulse buy! Make sure you know what to look for before leaving the house. Your shopping list should include the type of fabric, the exact amount you need and any colors or prints you think would go well with the design. Always buy your threads at the same time as your fabric – this way it's easier to make sure that the colors match exactly. If possible, take the pattern with you, because your local craft store will be able to offer advice if you are not sure what you need.

STANDARD FABRIC WIDTHS

Fabrics are sold in standard widths, which vary according to their purpose – for example, voile material for curtains is usually a different width to dressmakers' cotton cloth, which generally comes in standard widths of 36in (90cm) or 45in (115cm). However, some manufacturers use metric units and some use imperial, so a fabric measuring 36in will actually be a bit wider than 90cm. If this could make a difference to your project then we recommend carrying a tape measure and checking the figures for yourself. You will also see 'fat quarters' for sale. This is a quarter of a yard or meter of fabric, produced by cutting half a yard of fabric in half across the length. This gives you a piece of fabric about 18x22in or 45.5x56cm. Always double check you're buying the right amount of fabric.

mix & match

If you're new to embroidery, it's best to start off using plain colors rather than patterned fabrics. A plain block of color, especially in muted shades, will suit most designs and make sure your stitching is the part that stands out. Once you're more confident with embroidery and color, look around at some of the beautiful patterned fabrics available. Some fabrics with subtle patterns can look great with areas of embroidery!

Know your threads

Embroidery flosses are the most popular threads for embroidery but there are plenty of other options…

With a beautiful finish at a great price, embroidery flosses are the number one choice for embroidery projects. But if you venture beyond the world of flosses, you'll discover an amazing array of exciting threads to enjoy and experiment with! There are subtle linens, shiny satins, metallics and variegated embroidery flosses, as well as novelty options such as glow-in-the-dark, fluorescents and textured threads. You'll find there are all sorts of specialty embroidery threads, to suit every project, style and budget. Here's our guide to the threads that will stretch your stitching style.

Thread conditioner

Some speciality threads like fluorescents and satins can be tricky to stitch with due to their silky, slippery texture. Use shorter thread lengths to limit tangles. Some conditioners will also strengthen and protect your threads and make them easier to handle.

Linen

DMC Linen has a matte finish and comes in beautiful muted tones. It's perfect for any vintage-inspired projects. Remove the L from the color code to find the same color in normal embroidery floss.

Satin

Add a glamorous sheen to your stitching with DMC Satin threads. Each color has an embroidery floss equivalent, so they're simple to mix and match in any project that needs an extra special touch.

Hand dyed

For rich, vibrant hues, nothing beats hand-dyed thread. Be careful though, because hand-dyed threads aren't always colorfast.

Floche

Cotton floche is one of the highest quality embroidery threads out there. It has a high luster and is much softer than traditional embroidery floss.

Multicolor thread

For a unique, color-changing effect without any extra work, try out Anchor Multicolor thread. It's great for stitching flowers, lettering or any large block of color.

Fluorescent

When you really need your stitching to stand out, use DMC Fluorescent Effects threads. Try stitching a motif on black fabric for the ultimate color contrast!

Glow in the dark

This unassuming white thread from DMC glows green in the dark, making it perfect for leaving secret pictures and messages in your design that will only be seen once the lights go out. Kids will love it!

Perlé cotton

DMC Perlé cotton is a twisted thread, making it thicker than embroidery floss. Use just one strand instead of two to give your design a textured effect. It works well for free-hand embroidery and backstitch lettering.

Follow the simple instructions on each pattern to make lovely hand-embroidered creations!

Follow a pattern

Create your first embroidery project with our step-by-step guide to following pattern instructions for perfect results!

Embroidery projects tend to include instructions in various forms – such as written text, a chart, key and diagrams – to explain how to work the design.

The instructions should tell you what type of fabric you need and how much, where to place the design and where to start stitching. Usually, you start stitching at the center of the fabric, matching it to the center of the design. To find the middle of your fabric, fold it in half both ways, press down along the folds in the center, then mark the place where the fold lines cross with a pin. Use the same technique to find the center of

your design. Insert a pin through the center of the fabric and then the center of the paper template to line them up. Tape the two together with masking tape, then trace the design onto the fabric using the instructions on page 18.

The pattern should also give details of which threads you need to use. Most embroidery projects use embroidery floss and usually include color reference numbers for a particular manufacturer's range of embroidery flosses. The key manufacturers are DMC, Anchor and Madeira, and you can find conversion charts between their ranges on the internet. The instructions, chart or

diagram for a project should tell you which thread color to use in each area of the design. Once you're more confident with embroidery, you could mix and match your own shades of thread.

Finally, the instructions should tell you which stitches to use on different parts of the design. This is often shown on a chart or diagram and its key, which should also tell you how many strands of thread to use to form the stitches. Most stitches are formed using two strands of thread. If any of this information is missing from your pattern, refer to the photographs or just use the stitch, number of strands and colors that you think will work best.

Using templates

Most embroidery projects use templates, which you'll need to transfer onto your fabric to recreate the design. Here's how...

1 Before you start tracing, make sure your fabric is wrinkle free. Plan carefully where you want to place the design and make sure you leave yourself enough space. Check the project instructions for details of whether you need to enlarge your template on a photocopier. You can enlarge or reduce any design to suit your specific project.

2 The simplest way to transfer a design onto your fabric is to trace it. Hold the fabric right side up and place it over the template. Secure with masking tape so that it can't slip. Trace over all the lines using a pencil. If you struggle to see the design through the fabric, trace the design onto tracing paper using a fine black pen. Then tape the design and fabric to a window or a light box, and trace the design. To help with this, you could turn your fabric upside down and stretch it into a hoop or frame so that the right side of the fabric is in the back of the hoop and the wrong side is flush against the design surface. Make sure the template is easy to see and draw around it using a fabric pencil. Finally, remove the fabric from your frame and reinsert it right side up, ready to embroider.

3 If your fabric is too thick to do this or it's impossible to trace through the window, trace the design onto tracing paper and secure to your fabric with pins. Following your pencil lines, tack around the design using small, even stitches in a contrasting colored thread. Score along your tacking stitches with the tip of a needle and then remove the paper by simply tearing, and you're ready to go.

4 Alternatively, try dressmakers' carbon paper. First, trace the design onto plain paper. Cut a piece of dressmakers' carbon paper to fit the size of the design. Place the carbon paper over your fabric, where you want to place the design, with the dark side next to the fabric surface. Place your paper template on top and trace over the outline using a blunt pencil. Remove the carbon paper

and you will have created a dark outline for your embroidery design.

5 Once you've drawn your design onto the fabric, place it into a hoop. This will provide the correct tension; your stitches will be neater and it will prevent the fabric from puckering. If you're right-handed, work the embroidery stitches from right to left – if you're left-handed, work from left to right instead.

TRACE your picture directly onto your fabric using a washable or fading fabric pen, available at most craft and sewing shops.
PLACE dressmaker's carbon paper face down onto your fabric. Place your picture on top and trace using a blunt pencil.

PEAR
Template

Getting started

Starting a new project is the most exciting part!
Here's our quick guide to getting going with fabric and thread…

WASTE KNOT A simple way to get started with your embroidery.

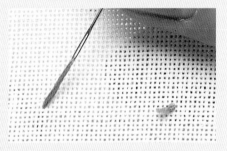

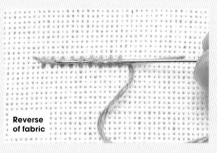

Step 1
Knot one end of your thread and take it down through the front of your fabric, about 2cm from your starting point. Bring it back up to make your first stitch.

Step 2
Begin stitching your design, making sure you stitch over your starting thread. Once your starting thread is secure, simply snip off the knot.

Step 3
To secure the thread when you've finished stitching, weave it through the back of your stitches (as shown above).

LOOP KNOT This easy start to your embroidery is brilliantly neat.

Step 1
If you're working in two strands, a loop knot is the easiest and neatest method. Cut a single length of thread and fold it in half to create a loop at one end.

Step 2
Thread your needle with the two tail ends. Bring your needle up to the front of your fabric, leaving a small loop of thread on the reverse.

Step 3
Make your first stitch and pass the needle through the loop on the reverse. Pull to secure the thread. Now continue with your stitching as normal.

SEAL YOUR FABRIC EDGES Simple ways to make sure your fabric won't fray.

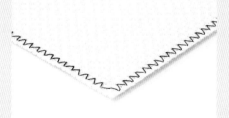

1 Masking tape
For a quick fix, seal edges with masking tape. It may leave a residue, so leave extra fabric around your design.

2 Blanket stitch
If you've got more time, use a blanket stitch to stop your fabric fraying. This can also be used for a decorative finish.

3 Zigzag stitch
For true security, use a sewing machine to stitch a quick zigzag right up to the edges. It's the best choice for linen.

Finishing your work

Follow our simple finishing techniques to ensure a professional result for your embroidery projects...

WASHING The washing stage can really bring your stitching to life.

Step 1
Before you start, check that your fabric and threads are colorfast and whether there are any specific washing instructions for them. Fill a tray with warm water and add a small amount of bleach-free detergent. Gently immerse your stitching in the water.

Step 2
Leave to soak for about 15 minutes, then gently agitate it in the tray. To remove frame marks, rub the fabric together at the edge, avoiding the stitches.

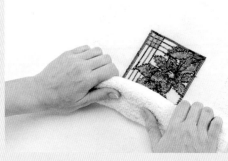

Step 3
For stubborn stains, empty your water. Place your stitching face up on the tray and use a sponge and fresh warm water to sponge that area.

Step 4
Rinse under warm water to remove the detergent. To remove excess water, roll your stitching in a white towel. Place face down on a towel to dry.

PRESSING For a smooth finish...
You may need to eliminate wrinkles from your finished piece with an iron. Pad your ironing board with a thick towel. Place your work right side down on top with a thin, clean cloth over it. Press carefully until the fabric is dry. The towel will stop the iron from flattening the stitches. Press gently, working the point of the iron into the stitches. Avoid having the iron too hot.

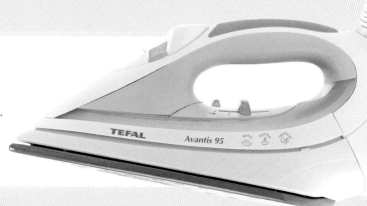

Embroidery stitches

The stitches you need for embroidery projects are very simple –
here are a few guides to start you off, while the rest start on page 24.

CROSS STITCH One of the simplest and prettiest embroidery stitches.

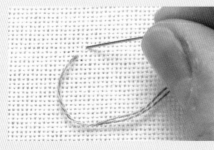 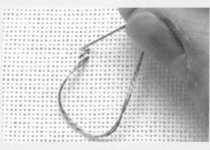 

Step 1
To start your stitching, take your needle diagonally across the fabric to form a half cross stitch – a short, straight line.

Step 2
Make a second diagonal stitch evenly in the opposite direction to complete one cross stitch.

Step 3
Continue working cross stitches like this to form the design. Make sure you cross each stitch in the same direction.

FRENCH KNOTS Go dotty with this simple way to add neat knots to your designs.

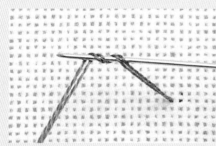 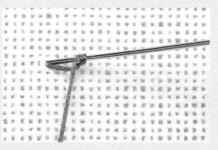 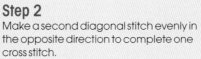

Step 1
Use a sharp embroidery needle to help pierce the fabric. Bring your needle up at your starting point and wrap your thread once or twice around the needle. Use one strand for a small knot and two for a slightly chunkier knot.

Step 2
Hold your thread end firmly and take your needle down, ever so slightly over from where you came up. Slide the twisted thread down the needle, so it rests on the fabric's surface, and gently feed the needle through the fabric.

Step 3
Keep your thread as taut as possible to prevent the knot becoming loose. Gently pull your thread through to tighten the knot, so that it sits neatly on the surface. And remember, if you don't get it right away, keep practicing!

BEADING

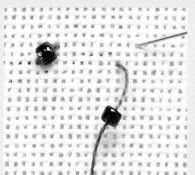

To attach beads, you'll need a thin, flexible beading needle. Thread the needle and bring it to the front of your design, thread on a bead and complete the stitch to secure the bead. If you like, stitch through the bead again for added security.

BACKSTITCH

Bring your needle to the front and make a small, straight stitch. For additional stitches, bring your needle up an even distance away from your previous stitch. Then pass it back through the fabric at the same point as your previous stitch.

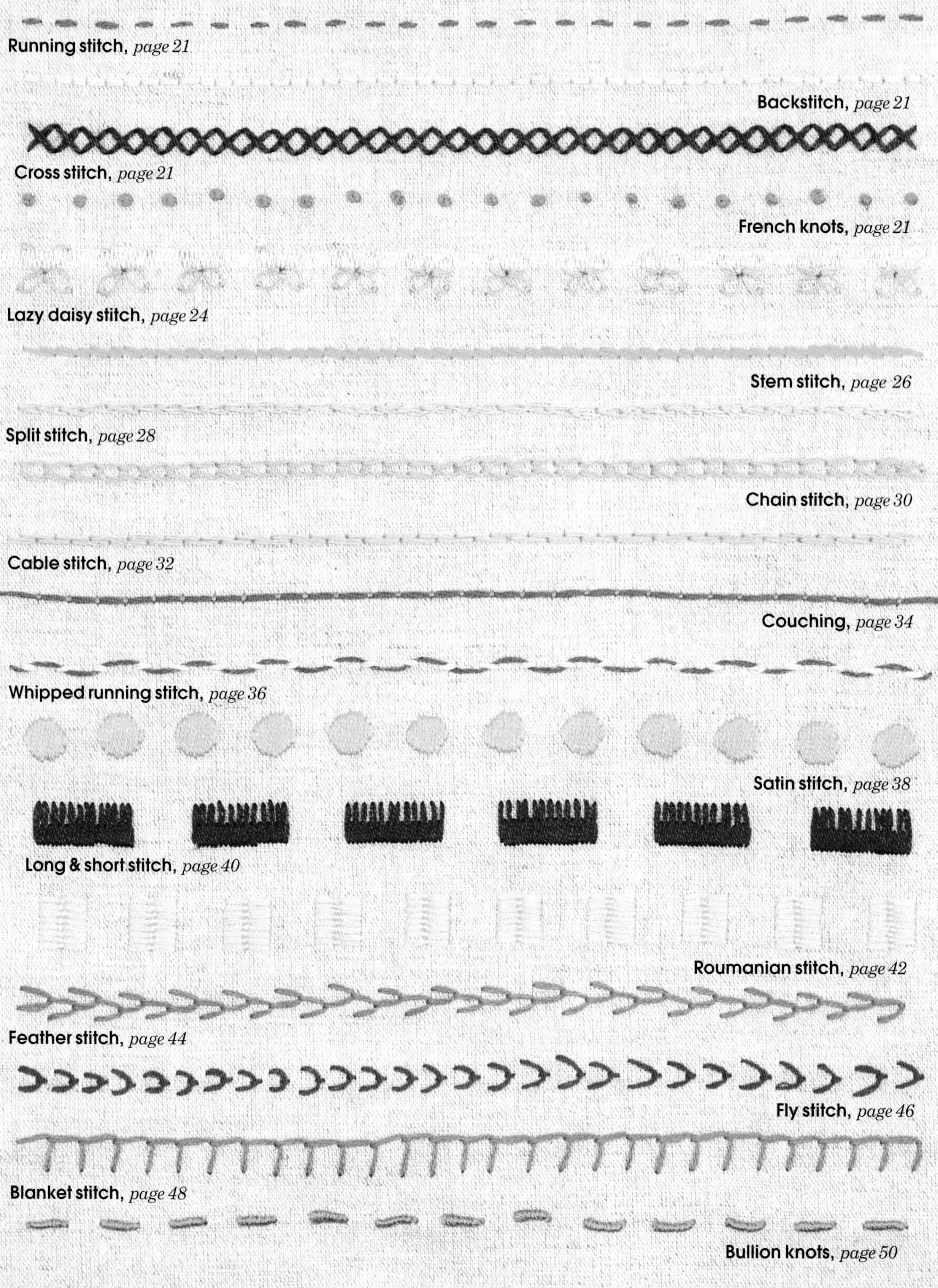

Running stitch, *page 21*

Backstitch, *page 21*

Cross stitch, *page 21*

French knots, *page 21*

Lazy daisy stitch, *page 24*

Stem stitch, *page 26*

Split stitch, *page 28*

Chain stitch, *page 30*

Cable stitch, *page 32*

Couching, *page 34*

Whipped running stitch, *page 36*

Satin stitch, *page 38*

Long & short stitch, *page 40*

Roumanian stitch, *page 42*

Feather stitch, *page 44*

Fly stitch, *page 46*

Blanket stitch, *page 48*

Bullion knots, *page 50*

Hand
embroidery projects

Lazy daisy stitch

designed by Diane Fortune

HOW TO WORK
LAZY DAISY STITCH

Bring the needle up and then
back down at the same spot to
form a loop, but don't pull the
thread all the way through. Bring
the needle up a short distance
from the center, pass it through
the loop, then back down where
it came up. This forms one petal.
Repeat to form a flower shape.

A favorite stitch for flowers, we've used a luxurious silk thread to create this pretty floral sachet design.

Lazy daisy stitch is very popular in embroidery
and can be used on all types of fabrics to
great effect. It is one of the easiest stitches to
learn and is great when used to represent flowers.
Lazy daisy stitches create instant flower petals and
they can be addictive – designer Diane Fortune says:
"I remember stitching lazy daisy flowers all over my
favorite dolls' clothes as a child!"

Lazy daisy stitches are also known as detached chain
stitches, because each stitch is formed from an individual
chain 'link' (see page 30 for more about chain stitch). We've
chosen an unusual thread for our bag – Kreinik Silk Serica
is a twisted thread used as one length. The pure silk has
a lovely sheen to it and is a pleasure to work with.

1 Transfer the image template to the
center of one piece of fabric (see page
18), then stitch the design as shown
opposite.

2 Place the fabric right sides together
and join around three sides,
leaving ¾in (2cm) at the top edge
unstitched.

3 Stitch a hem around the top.
Turn to right side and thread
through a ribbon as a drawstring.

TOP TIP
*The silk thread is quite twisty, so
make sure you work with short
lengths and let the needle and
thread dangle below your work
every so often to allow it to untwist.*

Simple but effective stitches

LAZY DAISY
Daisy circle
template

This is a great first embroidery project, using two simple stitches with luxurious thread to create a beautiful finished piece.

Use a contrasting color to work the French knots.

Using one strand of silk, start the lazy daisy flowers anywhere in the circle.

Carry on stitching around the circle, covering the pencil marks as you go.

When you've finished all the flowers, add French knots in the center.

Stem stitch

designed by Diane Fortune

It won't take long to make our stylish napkin using a simple stem stitch – a common stitch that's easy to work.

YOU WILL NEED

☐ A piece of surface embroidery linen – 16x16in (41x41cm), white

☐ Embroidery floss – color of your choice

☐ Crewel embroidery needle – size 8

☐ Sewing cotton – white

☐ Embroidery hoop

☐ Soft pencil or water soluble pen

☐ General sewing supplies, including scissors, needle, fabric marker, etc.

S tem stitch is one of the most popular outline stitches in embroidery. It's particularly good for using with curved lines and for emphasizing other stitches, and can also be effective when stitching lettering. It's a good idea to start practicing stitching in a straight line first, varying the length and angle of your stitches to see which style you prefer. Remember to work back on yourself, as shown below.

For our design, move your work around as you go so you are always working in the same direction. You will need to make smaller stitches when working around the curved edges of the knife and fork, to stop the thread from taking a short cut across the design. We chose to stitch our project on a piece of white surface embroidery linen, which is lovely to work with and gives a crisp finish.

Perfect for stitching outlines

HOW TO WORK STEM STITCH

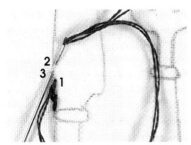

Bring the needle up just above the design line at 1, down at 2 below the line and back up at 3. Continue in this way, always working back on yourself, with point 3 always forming point 1 of the next stitch worked.

1 Transfer the template (right) onto your fabric, using the directions on page 18. We have used two strands of embroidery floss for this project. Choose your own color to stitch the napkin.

2 To start the stitching, bring your needle through the fabric to the front. Leave a 1in (2.5cm) tail on the back – this will be anchored under the first few stitches that you work.

3 Make sure that you cover all the lines as you stitch. Follow our picture guide (opposite), which shows you the direction and order to work in.

4 When you have finished all the stitching, wash your completed piece gently to remove any marks and to restore the crispness of the fabric. Immerse the stitched fabric in lukewarm water. If the color starts to run, just keep rinsing until the water runs clear. If there are any stubborn stains, rub a little light detergent on the area.

5 Pad your ironing board with a thick towel or two. Place your work right-side down on the board, then place a thin, clean cloth over it. Carefully iron until the fabric is dry. You can now hem your napkin, either by hand or machine.

Start by stitching the knife, working from left to right around the curves.

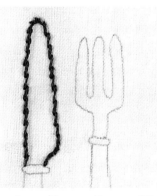

Focus on the outline and leave all the tricky details until last.

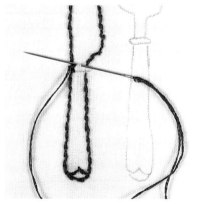

Now fill in the top of the handle. Work the fork in the same way as the knife.

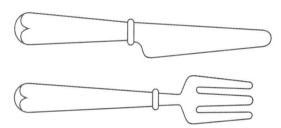

You could try using cable stitch to embroider this design – see page 32.

TOP TIP

As well as being ideal as an outline stitch for motifs, stem stitch is also very good to use for lettering. Why not add initials to the napkins for a great wedding or housewarming gift? Remember to always work in one direction and then work back on yourself.

STEM STITCH
Knife and fork template

YOU WILL NEED

☐ Cream muslin – enough to fit in your embroidery hoop

☐ Embroidery floss – bright green

☐ Embroidery needle – size 8

☐ Embroidery hoop

☐ Soft pencil

☐ Notebook – of your choice

☐ General sewing supplies, including scissors, double-sided tape, masking tape, sewing cotton, etc.

HOW TO WORK SPLIT STITCH

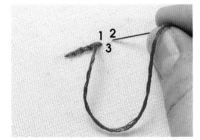

Bring the needle up at 1 and down at 2, then bring the needle up at 3, pulling it up through the center of the thread to split it. Make sure you always split the thread in the center to form even stitches. Point 3 will then become point 1 for the next stitch.

> **TOP TIP**
> *Take care when crossing over the lines in the 'joined up' areas, so that the thread lies flat and doesn't get knotted up below.*

Create this stylish notebook by using split stitch, which is great for embroidering outlines and lettering.

Outline stitches are invaluable in freehand embroidery, and split stitch gives a neat outline to any shape. It can also be used to fill areas when worked in rows close together. The finished look is similar to chain stitch, with the thread split to form small chain 'links'.

For this stitch, it's best to use a loosely twisted embroidery thread, which is easier to split. We've used embroidery floss, but crewel wool will also work well. You will need a sharp needle to split the thread neatly, otherwise your stitching will not follow an even line or curve, and the finished item may look a little scruffy.

Split stitch is quick to work and ideal for lettering – we've used it here to make a label for a notebook. You don't have to use our template though, you can take your alphabet from any source – look through the fonts on your computer and you'll find that script ones work well. Or use your own handwriting to make it even more individual. You could even use split stitch to embroider a friend's initials on a truly personalized gift!

Perfect for lettering!

Notes

SPLIT STITCH
Notebook lettering template

bright ideas!

♡

makes a **special present** for any occasion

♡

experiment with threads in different colors

♡

create a coordinating **greeting card**

1 Transfer the template (opposite) onto your fabric using the guide on page 18.

2 We used two strands of green embroidery floss for this project – you can choose your own thread color.

3 To start, bring your thread to the front of the fabric, leaving a small

tail on the back. Anchor this tail of thread under the first few stitches.

4 Stitch over the lines following the step-by-step guide below.

5 Cut your stitching ½in (1.5cm) larger than the finished label you'd like. Fold under the raw edges and work a

running stitch around the edges in a thread that matches your fabric.

6 Stick double-sided tape onto the back of your stitched fabric and place it on the book. Mark the position of the four corners with a pencil. Peel the backing off the tape, stick the fabric into position and erase the pencil marks.

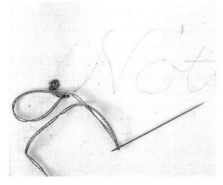

Start at the bottom of the letter 'N', following the pencil line. Stitch a double line where the lines cross.

Move on to the letter 'o', following the line to join onto the 't', just as you would when writing by hand.

Go back to cross the 't' when you've finished the 's'. Add the underline – you could use a second color.

- ☐ Green cotton fabric – enough to fit comfortably in your embroidery hoop

- ☐ Embroidery floss – green, brown and red, and gold metallic thread

- ☐ Embroidery needle – size 8

- ☐ Card – with a small decorative aperture, gold

- ☐ General sewing supplies, including scissors, tape, etc.

HOW TO WORK CHAIN STITCH

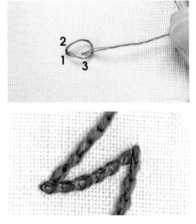

Work from right to left bringing the needle up at 1, down at 2 and up at 3, making sure that the loop of thread is under the needle. Pull the needle through slowly to form a neat loop – don't pull too tightly or the 'chain' effect will be lost.

Create all sorts of effects, outlines or lettering with this versatile stitch – try it out on our fab Christmas card!

Chain stitch is a great outline stitch, and works well when used decoratively as it curves easily. It also looks particularly effective stitched into spirals! Chain stitch works best if you make your stitches even, but they don't have to be small – in fact they look very effective when they're chunky. Here, we've combined it with some simple lazy daisy stitches (see page 24) to make a pretty Christmas tree.

Easy Christmas craft!

1 Transfer the template onto your fabric using the guide on page 18.

2 To start the stitching, bring your thread to the front of the fabric, leaving a tail at the back. Then anchor the tail under the first few stitches.

3 Follow the pencil line with your stitches and use the steps opposite to stitch each piece of the design. Make sure you stitch the green outline first, before the tinsel, to give the appearance of the trimming going around the tree.

4 Open out your card and place it face down on a table. Stick double-sided tape on the card around its opening, then place your stitching right side up on the table top. Turn the card over and center it over the design, then press the card firmly onto the fabric.

5 Secure the card by placing double-sided tape around the central section and on the edges of your fabric, and then pressing the far right piece of card onto it. Now your Christmas card is ready!

CHAIN STITCH
Christmas tree template

bright
ideas!

the ideal way to
bring a smile to
someone's face

try a bell or star
shaped aperture

use beads
instead of lazy
daisies for a
raised, 3D effect

*This card should
only take about
an hour to complete
- it's a great
last-minute craft!*

*You can use any type of
thread – you're only limited
by the size of your needle!*

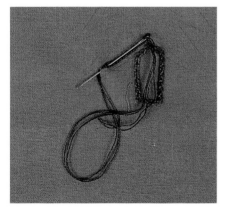

Start by working the tree trunk using
two strands of brown floss. Next add
the tree outline using dark green.

Now add the trimmings, using two
strands of the metallic gold thread
and overlapping the green outline.

Finally, add the hanging decorations
using single lazy daisy stitches and two
strands of red embroidery floss.

Cable stitch

designed by Diane Fortune

YOU WILL NEED

- ☐ Surface embroidery linen – 16x16in (41x41cm), white

- ☐ Embroidery floss – two colors of your choice (we've used green and orange)

- ☐ Crewel embroidery needle – size 8

- ☐ Embroidery hoop

- ☐ Hard pencil

- ☐ Sewing machine for hemming (optional)

- ☐ General sewing supplies, including scissors, pins, sewing needle, etc.

Another handy way to create outlines, cable stitch forms a lovely texture – use it to create this stylish napkin.

Outlining stitches are essential for embroidery and cable stitch is a great option for curves and for emphasizing natural details such as stems or small branches, because it gives a lovely raised and textured appearance. This charming design was inspired by a pretty Victorian bowl and pitcher set that Diane keeps in her dining room.

Neat alternative to stem stitch

HOW TO WORK CABLE STITCH

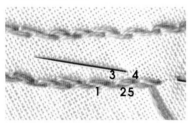

Work cable stitch from left to right by bringing the needle up through the fabric at 1, down at 2 and up at 3 in one movement. Push the needle down at 4, up at 5 and so on. It's important to keep the stitches the same length on both lines to give a neat, uniform appearance to your outline.

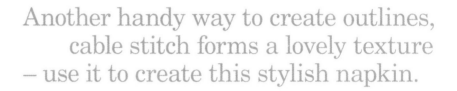

Start working in green at the left-hand side of the bowl and stitch left to right.

Next add the orange detail on the bowl, again working from left to right.

Start to outline the pitcher using the orange embroidery floss.

Finally, add the top lip of the pitcher, using green embroidery floss.

bright ideas!

♡
would look great as a **bathroom accessories** set

♡
change threads to match your **color scheme**

♡
combine with the **knife & fork** design on page 27

1 Transfer the template below onto your fabric using the guide on page 18.

2 All of the cable stitches are worked using two strands of embroidery floss. We have chosen pale orange and sage green colors for our bowl and pitcher design, but you can choose any two thread shades you like.

3 Work the cable stitch starting at the left-hand side and working to the right, paying attention to the length of the stitches and ensuring you keep them even. Follow the picture guide on the left to complete all the stitching neatly.

4 When you have finished all the stitching, press carefully, making sure the iron isn't too hot. Finally, hem your napkin using a hemming foot on a sewing machine, or by working a hand rolled hem using white sewing cotton.

CABLE STITCH
Bowl and pitcher template

This should only take a couple of hours to complete – make yourself a whole set!

Couching

designed by Diane Fortune

YOU WILL NEED

☐ Surface embroidery linen – two pieces 5x5in (13x13cm), cream

☐ Embroidery floss – lime green and burnt orange

☐ Crewel embroidery needle – size 8

☐ Embroidery hoop

☐ Soft pencil

☐ Cream sewing cotton

☐ General sewing supplies, including masking tape, tracing paper, pins, etc.

HOW TO WORK COUCHING

Place the thread to be couched onto a needle and bring it to the front of the fabric at the start of the stitching line, and hold it taut. Now bring the couching thread to the front of the fabric a little way along and make small, vertical stitches exactly the width of the couched thread. Repeat along the design lines to end of thread.

Couch our easy rooster egg cozy design to ensure a wide-awake start to the day, every morning!

Couching is traditionally used for goldwork embroidery to hold thick, metallic threads in place. It may look daunting, but you'll soon find that couching is surprisingly easy, as long as you remember to work small, vertical stitches and to make each of the stitches the same width as the laid thread, worked at equal intervals along it.

The nice thing about couching is that you can use any thickness or type of thread to couch down. Our rooster egg cozy design, for example, would work equally well with a sparkly knitting yarn and is a great way to use up left-over threads. Just remember to cover all the lines of your design accurately to produce a tidy outline.

Easy stitch with great results

1 Transfer the template onto your fabric using the guide on page 18.

2 For the laid thread, we have used six strands of embroidery floss, and then used two strands of embroidery floss for the couching thread.

3 To start stitching, use our photos and guides, opposite. Bring the thread to be couched up at a convenient place on the design. Remove the needle and hold the thread taut with your other hand.

4 Bring the couching thread up through the fabric a little way along the thread to be couched, and make a small, vertical stitch over the laid thread. Repeat to the end of the stitching line, and fasten off. Re-thread the couched

thread on your needle, take it through to the back of the work and fasten off.

5 Trace the egg cozy template outline onto your tracing paper, adding a ¼in (6mm) seam. Pin this over your stitched piece of fabric, making sure the design is central, and cut the fabric around the edge of the tracing paper. Repeat to cut out the backing fabric.

6 Pin the back and front pieces of fabric with right sides together and stitch around the curved edge using a ¼in (6mm) seam. Carefully turn right side out.

7 Turn under a ¼in (6mm) hem on the bottom edge of the egg cozy, pin carefully in place and then stitch a neat hem with small, invisible stitches.

Our egg cozy makes a great gift for the guys, or make a pair for a special couple!

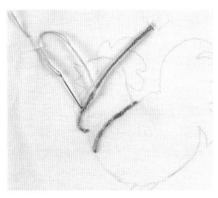

Lay your thread and start couching at a convenient place along the outline.

Make sure that your couching stitches are an equal distance apart.

Finish your cockerel with a French knot for his eye (see page 21 for details).

COUCHING
Egg cozy template

Whipped running stitch

designed by Diane Fortune

YOU WILL NEED

- ☐ Surface embroidery white linen – two pieces 11x7in (28x18cm)

- ☐ Embroidery floss – blue and green

- ☐ Embroidery needle – size 7

- ☐ Embroidery hoop

- ☐ Soft pencil

- ☐ Narrow ribbon – two pieces 21in (54cm)

- ☐ General sewing supplies, including scissors, masking tape, sewing cotton, etc.

HOW TO WORK WHIPPED RUNNING STITCH

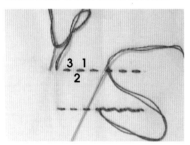

Work the running stitch, coming up at 1, down at 2, up at 3 and so on. For the whipping stitches, bring the needle up at the start of the line, then weave it through the running stitches. Always work from the top to the bottom.

Create a stylish bathroom bag by embroidering our simple seahorse with wavy whipped running stitches.

Whipped running stitch is a quick and simple way to embroider outlines, and it's ideal for creating these wavy lines! Running stitch is one of the easiest and most versatile embroidery stitches. It can be used to outline, to pad before working another stitch, or to attach a shaped piece of fabric, called appliqué.

We've made our seahorse more interesting by outlining him in whipped running stitch. The second thread won't go through the fabric, except when starting and finishing. Keep your running stitches the same length, but you can vary the space between the stitches.

Great stitch for beginners

1 Transfer the template opposite onto the center of one piece of your fabric, using the instructions on page 18.

2 To start the stitching, bring your threaded needle to the front of the linen where you want to start, leaving a small tail on the back – fasten this on the reverse under the first few stitches.

3 Work the embroidery following the step-by-step instructions opposite. We've used two strands of blue embroidery floss for the running stitch and two strands of green floss for the whipped stitches.

4 Place the two linen pieces right sides together, then sew along the base and sides, using a ½in (1.5cm) seam allowance. Neaten all the edges.

5 Fold the top over to form a 1in (2.5cm) hem. Sew a line of top stitching ½in (1.5cm) from the fold. Work another row of stitching ¼in (½cm) below.

6 Unpick the two side seams between the top stitching to create a small hole on either side. Thread one length of ribbon through the left hole, all the way around the bag and out through the same hole. Repeat for the other piece of ribbon, but thread it in and out through the hole on the right-hand side. Pull these ribbons to close the bag.

TOP TIP
You can use this design for all of your bathroom accessories. The stitching won't show up as well on towelling, but you could use stem or split stitch instead.

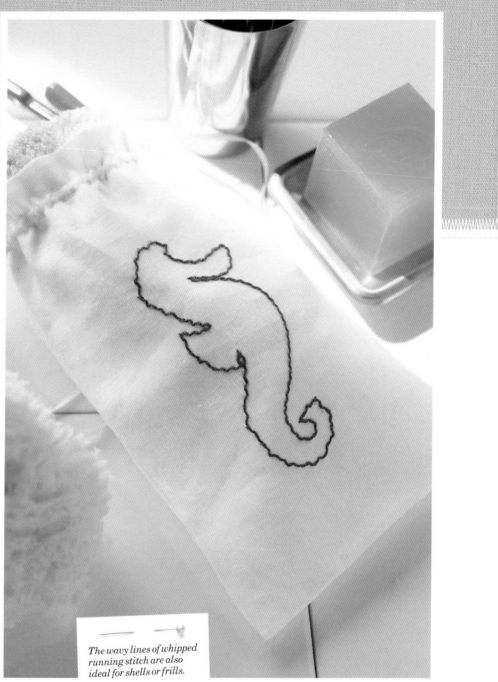

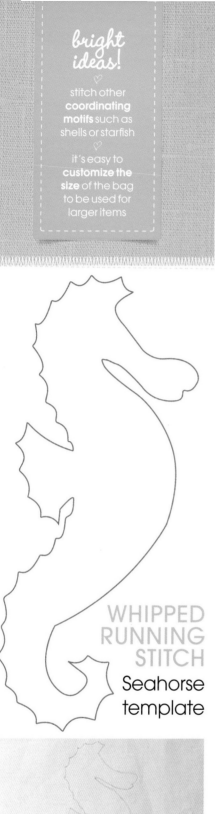

WHIPPED RUNNING STITCH

Seahorse template

The wavy lines of whipped running stitch are also ideal for shells or frills.

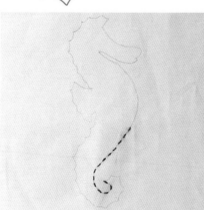

Start working the running stitch at a convenient place on the design. We started at the tail and worked up.

Work your way all around the seahorse outline, keeping your running stitches neat and even.

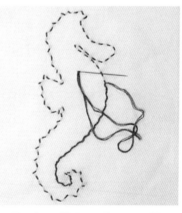

Work whipping stitches all around the design, weaving from side to side through the running stitches.

Satin

designed by ... Fortune

One of the most popular filling stitches, satin stitch is perfect for our simple daisy, shown off on a handbag mirror.

Satin stitch is one of our favorite stitches! It covers the fabric well and forms a smooth, even surface. It's worth slanting your stitches, as we've done here, so that light is reflected from the different areas in different ways – this can add interesting light and shadow effects to your design.

Super-simple filling stitch

1 Transfer the template below onto your fabric using the guide on page 18.

2 We have used two strands of embroidery floss for this project. You don't have to copy our colors – choose your favorites! You'll only need a tiny amount of the second color.

3 To start the stitching, bring your thread to the front, leaving a small tail at the back to be anchored under the first few stitches you work.

4 Follow the step-by-step guide opposite to stitch your flower. Make sure that you cover all the pencil lines. The direction of the stitches are indicated on the template by an arrow. You could add a French knot in the center, instead of satin stitches, if you prefer.

5 Carefully press the back of your stitched piece. Place the gold rim of the mirror over it, with the motif in the center. With a soft pencil draw round the outside of the rim.

6 Iron a piece of iron-on interfacing onto the back of the stitched piece. Now cut just inside the pencil line and fit your stitched piece in the rim of the mirror. Then follow the manufacturer's instructions to seal it together.

HOW TO WORK SATIN STITCH

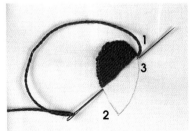

Bring your needle up at 1, down at 2 and back up at 3, ready for the next stitch. Keep the stitches close together, and under ¾in (2cm) in length.

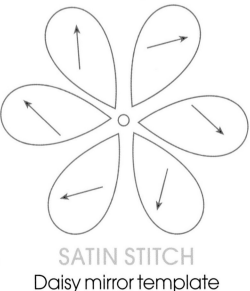

SATIN STITCH
Daisy mirror template

*Remember to work the stitches
at a different angle for each petal
– it creates interesting light
effects within your embroidery!*

*Use cotton in your favourite
flower shade – you could try
using white embroidery floss
and a colored fabric.*

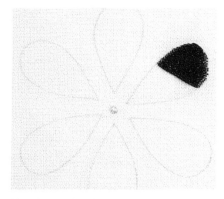

Start by working the three small satin
stitches in the center of the flower in
yellow, or your chosen color.

Now begin to stitch the petals in your
second color, following the direction
of the arrows on the template.

Draw around your mirror, iron a piece
of interfacing onto the back of the
fabric and carefully cut out the circle.

Long & short stitch

designed by Diane Fortune

PEAR PICTURE KEY
Use one strand of embroidery floss

DMC	Anchor	Color
580	267	Dark green
581	266	Green
780	310	Rust
3819	254	Light green

HOW TO WORK LONG AND SHORT STITCH

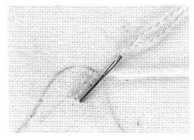

Work the first row using alternate long and short stitches. Work the following rows using long stitches, so that the top of each stitch goes into the row above it. Work the final row using just short stitches.

Learn how to use long and short stitches to create beautifully colored and textured motifs like this pretty pear.

Silk shading is a popular technique that gives brilliantly artistic results, using just the simple long and short stitch. As a variation on satin stitch, long and short stitches can fill any space with color, and the combination of stitches produces an attractive appearance that works brilliantly for shading colors together.

The technique is very straightforward and even beginners can do it. You just need a little practice and you'll soon be shading everything!

Use for a tonal, realistic effect

1 Transfer the template below onto your fabric using the guide on page 18. You don't need to transfer the arrows, as long as you note which way they are pointing. It may be best to trace the lines between each shade though, so that you know where to stop and start stitching.

2 We have used one strand of embroidery floss for this project – three toning greens and a rust color for the stalk.

3 Make sure that you cover all the lines of the design as you stitch. Follow our step-by-step guide (see opposite), which shows you the direction you need to work your stitches in. Imagine that you're using your needle in the same way you would use a coloring pencil, adding the shading to the design.

4 Start at the outside edge with long and short stitch. The inner section is filled with a second color.

5 When blending, there should be no straight edges or sudden changes of color, but the first row of stitches of the new color should slot between the last row of stitches of the previous one. In this way, you will get a gradual color change, which will make the finished design look more realistic.

6 Once done, press and frame your work – a rustic frame like we've used here complements it perfectly!

LONG AND SHORT STITCH
Pear motif template

Our pear would also look good if you simply outlined it using chain, split or stem stitch.

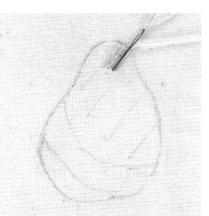

Start by marking the direction of the stitches and work the largest area first.

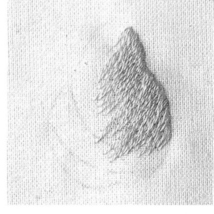

Fill in this area, then work the medium area, working into the lighter stitches.

Next, add the darkest shaded area. Finish off the pear by adding the stalk.

Roumanian stitch

designed by Diane Fortune

YOU WILL NEED

- ☐ Surface embroidery linen – 6x6in (15x15cm), cream

- ☐ Pearl cotton thread – black and yellow

- ☐ Embroidery needle – size 7

- ☐ Embroidery hoop

- ☐ Hard pencil

- ☐ Bias binding (optional)

- ☐ General sewing supplies, including scissors, pinking shears, pins, etc.

Your honey will taste even sweeter with this fun bee, combining Roumanian stitch and backstitch.

Roumanian stitch is another variation on satin stitch, which produces an attractive, raised strip – perfect for using down the body of our friendly bee! The stitch can be very useful in embroidery, because the length of the stitches can be altered to fill any shape.

The bee design for our honeypot cover is simple to work, but gives a sophisticated end result. Roumanian stitch gives the bee's vibrant stripes a gentle curve, so the body doesn't look too flat.

Simple textured filling stitch

HOW TO WORK ROUMANIAN STITCH

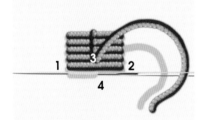

Bring the needle up at 1, down at 2 and up again at 3 midway between these two points – the thread should emerge just above the stitch just made. Take the thread over the stitch and push the needle down at 4 to make a short stitch. Alter the length of the long stitches to fit the desired shape but keep all the central stitches the same length and in a straight line.

1 Transfer the template opposite onto your fabric using the guide on page 18.

2 To start your stitching, bring the thread through the linen, leaving a small tail at the back – this will be anchored under the first few stitches.

3 Work the embroidery following the steps opposite. We have used one strand of pearl cotton throughout. Start by working the backstitch for the wings, extending slightly into the body area.

4 Work the Roumanian stitch, starting at the top edge with the black pearl cotton. Use the pencil lines as a guide and alter the length of stitches accordingly.

5 When you have finished all the stitching, press your work. We have frayed ¼in (6mm) around all the edges to finish. Your honey-pot cover can now be tied with ribbon or raffia to finish.

ALTERNATIVE FINISHING IDEAS

1 A quick way to finish your honeypot cover is to cut around the edge with pinking shears, or you can take a bit more time and finish your edge neatly with bias binding. Use a coordinated brightly colored binding, or try a gingham bias binding for fun.

2 Draw a circle around the design, then stitch a small zigzag border around this line using a sewing machine. Cut away the excess fabric and attach a piece of cotton lace to the edge.

3 Finish the edge of your honeypot cover by working a decorative machine stitch, or by cutting scallops and working blanket stitch edging.

4 Choose one of the pretty cutwork mats that are available in a similar size. They have a blank section in the center for you to stitch the design on.

Start by working the black backstitch for the bee's wings.

Next work the body in Roumanian stitch, starting with black pearl.

The pearl cotton thread we've chosen gives the finished piece a sheen that's very different from normal embroidery floss.

Then add the first stripe using yellow thread and Roumanian stitch.

Continue with the stripes, making sure you work the last few rows in black.

ROUMANIAN STITCH
Bee template

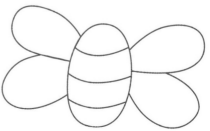

Feather stitch

designed by Diane Fortune

YOU WILL NEED

☐ Surface embroidery linen –
7½x9in (19x23cm), white

☐ Embroidery floss – yellow,
black and green

☐ Embroidery needle – size 8

☐ Embroidery hoop

☐ Hard pencil

☐ Frame – with a 3x4¼in
(7.5x11cm) aperture

☐ Batting – 3x4¼in (7.5x11cm)

☐ General sewing supplies,
including scissors, pins, etc.

Pretty and intricate, feather stitch is ideal for pictorial work – like our bright and colorful fish design!

Feather stitch is surprisingly easy to learn and creates a lovely, delicate texture. It can be worked in straight lines to add a decorative border, or in curved lines to add detail to pictorial work, as here. We've used feather stitch to represent the stripes on the fish as well as the seaweed. For the outline, we've used stem stitch – see page 26 for how to work this.

Creates delicate texture

HOW TO WORK FEATHER STITCH

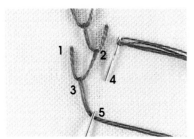

Bring the needle up at 1 and down at 2 to form a loop, but don't pull it through. Bring the needle back up at 3, keeping the thread under the needle. Make the next loop by pushing the needle down at 4 and up at 5, with the thread under the needle.

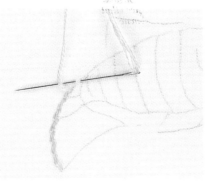

Start by outlining the shape of the fish in yellow using stem stitch.

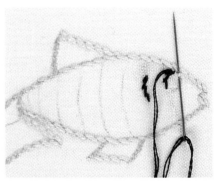

Next, add the other stem stitch details in black embroidery floss.

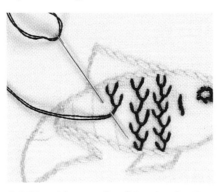

Add the stripes on the fish using feather stitch in black embroidery floss.

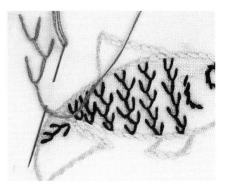

Finally, add the feather stitch seaweed using two strands of green floss.

bright ideas!

♡

quirky gift for a **swimmer** or fish lover!

♡

would look great **edging a towel** or wash cloth

♡

great for using up **odds and ends** of thread

1 Transfer the template below onto your fabric using the guide on page 18.

2 For the feather stitch, we've used two strands of green or black embroidery floss. For the stem stitch, we used two strands of black or yellow embroidery floss. To start your stitching, bring the thread through to the front of the linen, leaving a small tail at the back – this will be anchored under the first few stitches. Finish each thread by weaving the needle under the last few stitches.

3 Work the embroidery as shown in our step-by-step guide, left. Use our guide to feather stitch to get the work just right. We've used larger loops in the stitches for the seaweed, for a more open look. We've also curved the lines to give the seaweed movement.

4 Your stitched piece is now ready to be framed. Turn to page 20 for instructions on how to wash and press your piece for a perfect finish. When choosing a frame, think about where your picture will go. This cheery fish is ideal for a bathroom and the translucent frame adds an underwater feel!

5 To frame your stitching, place some batting between the fabric and the frame's backing board for a nice, plump look. Pin the fabric to the center of backing board, making sure it's taut in all directions, then carefully 'lace' up the back of the fabric to hold it in place, using a sharp needle and white thread.

A translucent frame allows you to see the edges of the stitching, to great effect!

TOP TIP
Feather stitch is also great for adding borders to any embroidered work – try combining it with one of our other projects.

FEATHER STITCH Fish template

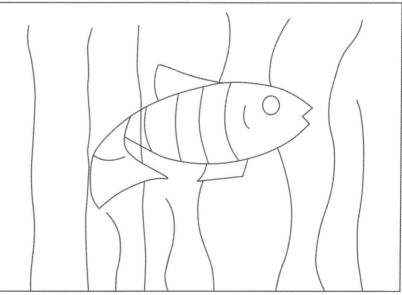

HOW TO WORK
FLY STITCH

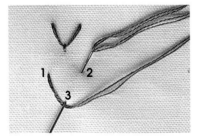

Bring the needle up at 1, then down at 2, without pulling the needle through the fabric. Come up again at 3, over the thread of the first stitch, and pull it through. Make a short, horizontal stitch to secure the 'V' shape of the stitch.

Use simple, easy-to-learn fly stitches to create this pretty sachet – perfect for keeping kitchen drawers fresh!

Fly stitch is a very versatile stitch that can be used in rows to make a decorative border, or worked in columns for a totally different look. It can also be used as an isolated stitch worked randomly across a design for a quirky feel!

Here, we have used fly stitch in rows to represent the sprigs of rosemary, with some backstitch writing to finish.

Great stitch for borders

1 Transfer the template (right) onto your fabric using the guide on page 18, placing it 2½in (6.5cm) from the top.

2 We used two strands of floss for the fly stitch, and one strand for the backstitch lettering. To start your stitching, bring the thread through the linen, leaving a small tail on the back and anchor it under the first few stitches.

3 Use the step-by-step guide opposite to stitch the rosemary sprigs over your traced template, one line at a time. Then add the backstitch lettering using one strand of very dark green floss.

4 Fold the linen in half, with right sides together. Sew up both sides using a ½in (13mm) seam allowance.

5 Turn the sachet to the right side. Fold the top over to form a ¼in (6mm) double hem and stitch in place.

6 Now place your rosemary inside and tie the top with the length of ribbon.

FLY STITCH
Rosemary template

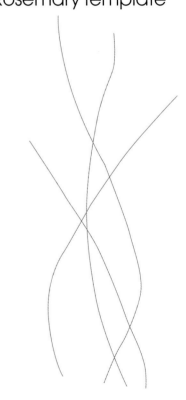

So quick and simple to make – finish one in an evening!

Use a pencil to write out 'Rosemary' below the sprigs before backstitching it.

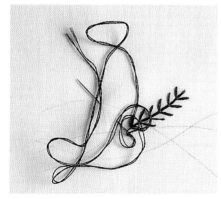

Start at the top of each line with one long stitch before your first fly stitch.

Continue with the fly stitch until all the lines of sprigs are completed.

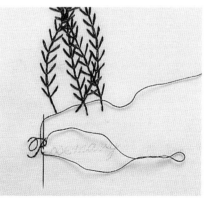

Add the lettering using backstitch and starting with the letter 'R'.

Blanket stitch

designed by Diane Fortune

YOU WILL NEED

- ☐ Surface embroidery linen – 7x7in (18x18cm), cream

- ☐ Embroidery floss – light green and dark green

- ☐ Embroidery needle – size 7

- ☐ Frame – with a 3¼x3¼in (8x8cm) aperture, wood

- ☐ Batting – 3¼x3¼in (8x8cm)

- ☐ Paints/pencil crayons (optional)

- ☐ General sewing supplies, including scissors, pencil, embroidery hoop, etc.

Blanket stitch is a great border stitch, but it can also be used in other creative ways, like with this leaf!

You'll recognize blanket stitch from the dainty edges of pretty pillowcases or the chunky edging of wool blankets. Blanket stitch was traditionally used to stop edges from fraying, but it also makes a great decoration and is often used in appliqué to attach fabric shapes. Here, we've used it as an outline stitch so you can get some practice.

Creative and versatile stitch

HOW TO WORK BLANKET STITCH

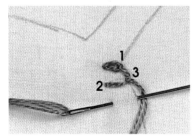

Make a chain stitch or other stitch to secure your thread. Bring the needle up at 1, down at 2 and up at 3 with the thread under the needle. Gently pull the needle through to form a neat loop. The vertical stitches should be evenly spaced and the same length.

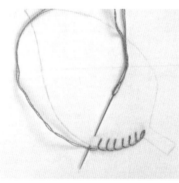

Start stitching at a convenient place on the design, such as by the stem.

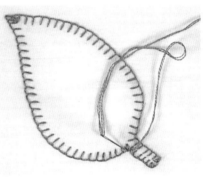

You'll need to make your stitches shorter at the stem, to fit them in.

You can add stem stitch for the vein. Turn to page 26 for full instructions.

Stencil a reduced version of the leaf onto your frame and assemble.

1 Start by transferring the template (below) onto the linen fabric, following the instructions on page 18.

2 We've used two strands of embroidery floss for this project. You can choose your own colors for the leaf design – you'll just need a light green and a dark green color that work well together.

3 To start stitching, first bring your threaded needle to the front of the fabric. Leave a small tail of thread on the back – make sure you anchor the tail under the first few stitches.

4 The pencil line you've drawn will show the outer edge of the design. You may find it helps to draw another line on the fabric, inside and parallel to the outline. This will help you to keep the length of the stitches consistent, but you'll need to wash off this pencil line when you're finished.

5 Now use the step-by-step guide (left) to blanket stitch the leaf design onto the linen fabric.

6 To decorate your frame in the same way as we have, reduce the template to fit the width of the frame – the easiest way to do this is by using a photocopier, but you could draw this out by eye.

7 Transfer the leaf to a piece of card and then carefully cut out the inside of the leaf shape using a craft knife. This will create a stencil you can work with. Stencil directly onto the frame using your template and light green paint or pencil crayon. Once dry, add the vein line on top in dark green. We've matched the thread colors so the frame and picture work together.

Stencil a smaller version of the leaf around your frame for a coordinated look.

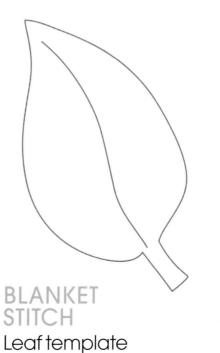

BLANKET STITCH
Leaf template

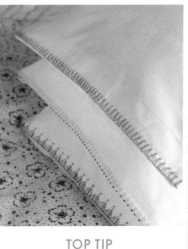

TOP TIP
You can create some artistic effects by varying the length of your blanket stitches, the distance between them or adding beads. We love these blanket stitch pillowcases from Jane Brocket's new book, The Gentle Art of Stitching.

Bullion knots

designed by Diane Fortune

Learn to stitch stylish bullion knots with our easy step-by-step guide and make this delightful daisy card.

YOU WILL NEED

☐ Muslin fabric – 16x16in (41x41cm), natural

☐ Pearl cotton – gold, yellow and jade

☐ Embroidery needle – size 7

☐ Embroidery hoop

☐ Card – with a 4½x3in (11.5x7.5cm) opening, yellow

☐ General sewing supplies, including scissors, pencil, etc.

HOW TO WORK BULLION KNOTS

Bring the needle up through the fabric and make a backstitch. Now bring the needle up again at your starting point, but don't pull the needle all the way through. Wrap the thread around the tip of the needle as many times as required. Holding the twists firmly with your thumb, pull the needle up through both the fabric and the coil of thread. Pull back over the backstitch so that the coil lies flat on the fabric. Take the needle through to the back of the fabric.

Similar to French knots, bullion knots are long, coiled stitches that can be used on almost any type of fabric and can be worked to any length. They can take a little practice to perfect but it's well worth persevering for the stunning three-dimensional results.

Creates striking texture

1 Transfer the template onto your fabric using the instructions on page 18.

2 All of the embroidery is worked using one strand of the pearl cotton thread. You might want to try using a gold-plated needle to work the bullion knots, because it will slip through the coiled thread more easily. Make sure your needle isn't too thin, though – with bullion knots, the thread needs to be pulled through the center of the coils, so if your needle is too thin, the coils will be too small.

3 Stitch the daisy following the photos and guide opposite. Start by working the stem stitch details using the jade thread. Turn to page 26 for full instructions on how to work stem stitch.

4 Now add the satin stitch flower center using one strand of gold thread. You will find instructions on how to work satin stitch on page 38.

5 You're now ready to add the bullion knot petals using the yellow thread. Start at the end of each line next to the central circle and work to the outside, following our instructions.

6 Once you've finished, mount your daisy in a card. To do this, place small strips of double-sided tape around the aperture, then carefully center the stitching and press into place.

BULLION KNOTS
Daisy template

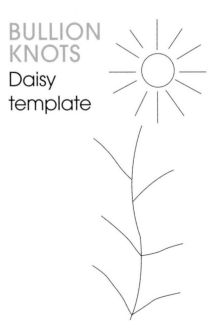

bright ideas!

♡

try working several bullion knots in a circle to create a **delicate rose**

♡

repeat the daisy design around a **tablecloth** or **pillowcase**

Once you've perfected bullion knots, try using them to make other flowers.

Start by working the leaves in stem stitch, then stitch the center stem.

Next, carefully work the center of the daisy using satin stitch.

Finally add the flower's bullion knot petals all around the satin stitch circle.

Eye mask

designed by Rebecca Preston

Ensure a peaceful night's sleep using our pretty mask, created with a combination of fabric and stitching.

YOU WILL NEED

- ☐ Small pieces of polka-dot fabric, in a variety of colors

- ☐ Embroidery floss – green, blue, orange and pink

- ☐ Crewel embroidery needle

- ☐ Cardboard – 8x5in (20x12cm)

- ☐ Batting – 8x5in (20x12cm)

- ☐ Two pieces of thin ribbon

- ☐ Fabric scissors

- ☐ General sewing supplies, including masking tape, pencil, pins, etc.

Embroidery designs on any fabric create a beautiful effect, but are you looking for some ideas that involve stitching on something a bit different to the usual plain white or cream cotton? Why not try stitching directly onto a variety of printed fabrics instead? Just swap your plain linens for some gorgeous patterned fabrics and start stitching! It's a great way to ensure plenty of color in your creations, without having to cover every bit of the fabric. Polka dots, large or small, are the perfect place to start and they're easy to embellish with simple cross stitches or lazy daisies. Once you get going, you could add beads and French knots for even more appeal.

Combine patchwork and embroidery!

---

3 WAYS... STITCHING *on* FABRIC *Here are a few ideas to get your creative juices flowing*

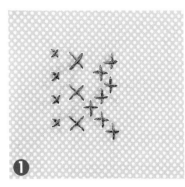

❶ FOR TINY polka dot fabric, just play join the dots and stitch crosses or other shapes in any size or direction!

❷ WORK ACROSS just one gingham square or several, as shown here, to create a more varied effect.

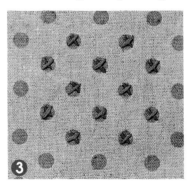

❸ ON FABRIC with large dots, the quickest way to add personality is by stitching inside each dot.

*Try using elastic
instead of ribbon for
the fastening.*

1 Create a mask template on a piece of
cardboard. Ours is about 8in (20cm)
long. Trace onto the reverse of your fabric.
If you like, sew two or three small fabric
pieces together instead of one piece.

2 Before doing any cutting, add your
stitching. Add cross stitches over
some of the polka dots. For some of the
smaller polka dots, try adding French
knots or even beads to the center.

*Use a variety of sewing
and embroidery skills to
create this stylish mask,
which is perfect for
ensuring a great night's
beauty sleep!*

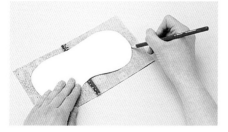

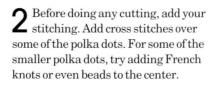

3 Cut out your stitched piece, plus a
backing piece and a piece of batting,
all to about ½in (1.5cm) beyond the
tracing line. Layer the fabric pieces right
sides facing, with the batting on top.

4 Sandwich a length of ribbon between
your stitched piece and the backing
piece, on both sides. Pin and sew, leaving
an opening for turning. Turn and slip
stitch the opening closed to finish.

TOP TIP

*A selection of patterned fabrics,
sewn together to create a patchwork
effect, make a great base for this type
of embroidery. The different prints
will inspire different types and
colors of stitching, so you'll create
a piece that's fun to stitch and
a joy to look at!*

YOU WILL NEED

☐ Surface embroidery linen, two pieces 30x22in (74x54cm), white

☐ Embroidery floss, as listed in the key

☐ Crewel embroidery needle – size 8

☐ Ribbon, 1in (2.5cm) wide, 11 feet, 6in (3.5m) long

☐ Embroidery hoop

☐ Casing strip, 22x2in (54x5cm)

☐ General sewing supplies, including scissors, pins, washable fabric marker, etc.

L et's face it, nobody likes spending precious hours that they could be devoting to their embroidery doing the laundry! And when your nearest and dearest prefer to leave a long, winding trail of clothes from the bedroom to the bathroom, it doesn't make life any easier.

Actions often speak louder than words, so embroider Sue's laundry bag and the message may just sink in. If you make something that looks fun, eye-catching and practical, you could find your wasted time (and your backache) reduced considerably when laundry day comes around again!

1 Transfer the design (on page 57) onto your fabric, using our guide on page 18. Embroider the design first – you'll make up your laundry bag afterwards. Both the large and small designs are stitched in one strand of embroidery floss. Refer to the color diagram as you embroider.

2 All the outlines are stitched first using backstitch. Next, fill in the main solid-colored areas using satin stitch. The little black cat is stitched using long and short stitch, to give an authentic 'furry' effect! Once you've finished him, embroider all the tufts of grass using long stitch. Now work the washing line posts, border of the tea towel, cuffs and waistband of the pajamas, apron strings, stripy nightshirt, bra and waistband of the blue spotty bloomers using rows of backstitch.

3 Now make up your laundry bag using this handy method, which will work with any drawstring bag. Put the front and back of the bag right sides together and sew around the bottom and sides, allowing for a ½in (13mm) seam allowance. Fold the top of the bag over by ½in (13mm), pin and hem down.

4 Now attach a 2in (5cm) casing strip to the bag. Place it roughly a quarter of the way down from the top of the bag, on the wrong side of the fabric.

5 Cut your length of ribbon in half and make a small slit in the casing at both sides of the bag. Start at the left-hand side and thread the ribbon all the way round and out of the same hole. Knot the two ends together. Repeat for the right-hand side and you're done!

TOP TIP
You can reduce or enlarge the design to suit you. Just remember to use a bigger or smaller piece of fabric! If you make the design bigger, stitch it using a thicker thread such as pearl cotton no 8. You could also use extracts from the pattern, to make smaller items, just as we've done with the little sachet.

bright ideas!

♡

change the **colors and patterns** to match your home

♡

ensure the **threads are colorfast** if it's likely to get washed!

There's no excuse for not keeping your laundry neat and tidy with this bag – it's colorful, fun and does the job perfectly!

Just four simple stitches are used to give a hand-drawn touch to the whole design.

Stitch the grass in long stitch over the cat to give a 3D feel to the whole scene.

Add some dried lavender to your embroidered sachet to help keep moths at bay.

Color	DMC	Anchor	Madeira
Mauve	209	109	0711
Black	310	403	Black
Grey	317	400	1714
Turquoise	597	1064	1110
Brown	612	832	2108
Pink	718	088	0707
Orange	741	304	0203
Yellow	743	302	0113
Blue	798	146	0911
Green	3819	278	2703

Use one strand of embroidery floss unless otherwise stated.

MATCHING SACHET

Keep all your laundry fresh until the moment you want to wear it with this matching lavender pouch. Sue's taken two items from the clothesline and embroidered them onto a little sachet. It's a perfect quick project if you're short on time.

To make the bag, take two pieces of white linen measuring 6x5in (5x12.5cm). Transfer your design onto the fabric and embroider following the main instructions. We stitched two pairs of bloomers from the main washing line, but you could stitch the black cat instead if you prefer.

Now make up your sachet in the same way as described for the laundry bag on the previous pages. Note that in step 3, your casing strip needs to be 1in (2.5cm) wide. Once you're finished, just fill your bag with lavender and pop it in your drawer.

TOP TIP
This design would also look stunning in a monochrome style for an ultra-modern look. Or why not tweak the clothes on the line to match your family's laundry – whether your clothesline is filled with band T-shirts or cloth diapers, you can make this pattern your own!

pegs

LAUNDRY BAG
Template

Use overlapping lines of backstitch, highlighting rather than filling in the wood, to help create a textured, realistic grain on your clothesline posts.

Bright buttons

designed by Lesley Teare

With just a few colorful strands, any button will soon blossom with these bright and blooming wonders!

YOU WILL NEED

☐ Muslin – enough to work the amount of buttons you need

☐ Embroidery floss – colors listed in the key

☐ Self-cover buttons in 1in (29mm) and 1½in (38mm)

☐ Crewel embroidery needle – size 8

☐ Items to add buttons onto

☐ General sewing supplies, including scissors, tape, tracing paper, pins, etc.

Add a small touch of hand-stitched color to any outfit or accessory with Lesley Teare's beautiful flower buttons. These miniature designs have a delicate elegance that would look gorgeous embellishing any fashion or homeware items. The patterns are great for beginners as well as more experienced stitchers, who might like to experiment with different sized buttons and fabrics.

"The scope is endless and by creating these button designs, you are making your own very personal stamp," says Lesley. So, grab that needle, get stitching and impress your friends, colleagues and family with your glorious accessories!

Small, fast projects

The buttons would look fab edging a quilt or duvet cover. Or use a darker background fabric for more 'manly' buttons for him.

1 Transfer the templates (page 60) onto your fabric using our guide on page 18. Allow 1x1in (2.5x2.5cm) for each design.

2 Place your fabric in a hoop and begin stitching. Use two strands of crewel wool for the French knots and satin stitch, and one strand of crewel wool for the stem stitch and long stitch. This design was originally stitched using Appleton's crewel wool, but we've included a conversion to embroidery floss if you prefer to use these – just use three strands of embroidery floss instead of one strand of crewel wool.

3 Wash and press your stitching (see our guide on page 20), then mount onto the self-cover buttons following the manufacturer's instructions.

4 If you want to make the cushion (as shown opposite), you'll need to sew your buttons on after you have placed the cushion pad inside the cover. Use extra strong (button or quilting) thread and take the needle in at the back and through to the front, going completely through the cushion pad for a quilted effect. Thread the button onto the needle and take the thread to the back. Make a second stitch in the same way, then secure and fasten off.

TOP TIP
These small, neat floral designs would also look great stitched around the edge of a cushion cover or tablecloth.

Brighten up any plain or neutral item with our vibrant embroidered buttons.

Color		Appleton Crewel Wool	DMC	Anchor		Color		Appleton Crewel Wool	DMC	Anchor
	light grass green	251A	734	279			peacock	832	3815	208
	grass green	254	732	281			custard yellow	851	745	300
	mid bright mauve	452	553	097			coral orange	862	722	323
	bright mauve	455	3837	101			coral red	866	900	326
	autumn yellow	473	728	306			pale hyacinth	891	3747	342
	pale rose pink	751	818	1020			mid hyacinth	894	3807	118
	dark rose pink	756	3731	076			dark hyacinth	895	158	119

bright
ideas!

♡

stitch someone's
favorite flower
onto a card

♡

**vary the thread
colors** for a more
muted look

♡

great for using
up spare **scraps
of thread**

*Enlarge the designs slightly to make
larger buttons - or stitch them even
bigger for great greetings cards or
gift tags for a special occasion.*

STRAWBERRY
Work the coral red satin stitch for
the berry first, then autumn gold
satin stitch seeds on top. Create the
stalk in grass green stem stitch.
Finally, work the satin stitch leaves
in light grass and grass green.

BLACKBERRY
Work the satin stitch berry in
bright mauve. Add leaves in satin
stitch in light grass green. Stem
stitch the stalk using grass green.
Add French knots on top in mid
bright mauve thread.

MARIGOLD
Work the satin stitch petals using
autumn gold thread. The center of
the flower is then worked in satin
stitch using a light grass green,
with an outline of French knots in
coral orange.

PANSY
Work autumn yellow, custard
yellow and bright mauve satin
stitch petals. Add coral orange long
stitch. Work the long stitch and
French knot in peacock.

*Go color crazy with
these fantastic motifs by
jazzing up your wardrobe
and furnishings - colorful
buttons make any ordinary
item look special!*

COLUMBINE
Work the stem in grass green stem
stitch. Add satin stitch petals in
bright or mid bright mauve. Stem
stitch the tops in mid bright mauve.
The long stitch leaf is in grass green.

TULIP
Work the satin stitch petals in coral
red. Work the long stitch in grass
green or autumn gold. Finally,
embroider the stem using long
stitch in grass green.

POPPY
Work the satin stitch petals in coral
red. The center is worked in satin
stitch using light grass green.
Outline the center in French knots
using bright mauve.

BRIAR ROSE
Work petals in satin stitch using
pale rose pink. Add the long stitch
in two strands of grass green and
mid rose pink. Finally, work the
French knots using autumn gold.

LILY

Work the satin stitch petals using pale rose pink, then do the stem in grass green stem stitch. The long stitch on the flower head is in dark rose pink and grass green. Work the French knots in dark rose pink.

BUTTERFLY

Work the butterfly's wings in satin stitch using autumn yellow and mid rose pink. Then add the long stitch and stem stitch in dark rose pink and finish with a French knot in the same color.

BUMBLE BEE

Work satin stitch stripes of dark hyacinth and autumn yellow, then the wings in mid and pale hyacinth satin stitch. Work the long stitch and French knots in mid hyacinth.

CORNFLOWER

Satin stitch the petals in dark and mid hyacinth. Add long stitch in two strands of dark hyacinth. Satin stitch the stem in light grass, then long stitch in peacock over the top.

SNAIL

Work the shell in satin stitch using custard yellow. Add the body in satin stitch using autumn yellow. Finally, work the shell details using split stitch in autumn yellow.

Baking book cover

designed by Susie Johns

Become a domestic goddess by creating our baking book cover, then enjoy dreaming up recipes to fill the pages.

YOU WILL NEED

- ☐ Gingham fabric in blue and white, to cover your notebook (we used 12x20½in/31x52cm)

- ☐ Embroidery floss and Anchor Marlitt, as listed in the key

- ☐ Ribbon – narrow green and white gingham for lettering

- ☐ Embroidery needle – size 9

- ☐ Beads in red and white

- ☐ Ring-bound notebook with a front cover at least 10¼x6¼in (26x16cm) in size

- ☐ General sewing supplies, including scissors, pins, washable fabric marker, etc.

EXTRA TREATS

If you don't want to start with the book cover straight away, have a go at making something smaller. Susie has embroidered one of her delicious strawberries on a card to accompany the book project. But any of the motifs would look good on their own. Why not create some matching accessories?

'Color in' design with satin stitch

Colorful cakes, berries and sugary flowers decorate the cover of this charming book, which is sure to win the heart of every crafty cook. The bright cake motifs are really easy to stitch and guarantee to have your mouth watering in seconds! In contrast, the more detailed padded satin stitch creates a rich, textured effect, which is further enhanced by adding ribbons and beads.

1 Mark the area on your fabric that will be the front of the book. We marked 4in (10cm) and 10¼in (26cm) from the right-hand edge, then 1in (2.5cm) from the bottom and top edges. Trace the template from page 64 centrally onto this area, following our guide on page 18.

2 You can work this design in any order, so pick your favorite part – or the easiest – and start with that first. Follow the template on page 64 to choose the stitches and colors to use for each part of the design. For the padded satin stitch areas, just cover the space roughly in chain or stem stitch first, then satin stitch over the top for a raised effect. Do all the embroidery using two strands of embroidery floss, and work all the motifs before the lettering. Use the rayon thread to give the flowers a lovely sheen.

3 When you're ready to stitch the lettering, start by laying on strips of the ribbon and catching them down. You will need to make a little fold at each end

of the ribbon to ensure it stays neat. You can then finish the lettering using more padded satin stitch.

4 Take your hardback ring-bound notebook, 10¼x6¼in (26x16cm) or bigger. Open out the notebook and lay your gingham fabric over it with the design on the front cover. Make sure there's 1in (2.5cm) extra fabric at the top and bottom edges, and an extra 4in (10cm) of fabric for the front and back flaps. Push pins around the edges of the cover to hold the fabric in place and close to make sure it fits properly.

5 Neaten the edges with a double hem at the top and bottom. Then hem the two short edges and fold over the flaps. Now slip stitch the flaps in place, attaching to the front and back covers.

6 Slip the flaps over the notebook and close to finish. Now to fill the book with delicious family recipes…

bright ideas!

♡

mix and match the motifs

♡

stitch **bold outlines** in a darker thread

♡

try adding some **appliqué** as well

Use the red beads to create super-juicy raspberries that really stand out!

Anchor	DMC	Madeira
Use two strands of embroidery floss		
White		
01	white	white
Coral		
11	350	0410
Red		
13	347	0211
Sugar pink		
66	3608	0709
Pale blue		
159	800	1002
Dark grey		
236	413	1713
Green		
256	704	1308
Lemon		
295	726	0109

Anchor	DMC	Madeira
Use two strands of embroidery floss		
Gold		
311	3855	2301
Apricot		
336	352	0302
Pale grey		
900	3072	1709
Rose pink		
1021	761	0813
Anchor Marlitt or other rayon thread		
Use one strand		
Purple		
819		
Gingham ribbon		
Attach using one strand of green thread		
Green and white		

Notebook cover

designed by Rebecca Preston

Give a traditional apple motif a cheeky twist with an adorable little worm poking out!

1 Trace the template onto a square of plain fabric such as muslin. Use stem stitch for the red apple outline and backstitch for the leaf, worm and stem.

2 To make an A5 (8.3x5.8in) notebook cover, take your piece of linen, fold in the short edges by 1in (2cm) and hem. Fold in the long edges by about 1in (2cm) and press.

3 Fold in each short edge by 3in (8cm) and work a red running stitch at the edges to secure. Fold under the edges of your stitched patch by 1in (2cm) and stitch onto the front of the notebook cover using red running stitches. Insert the A5 (8.3x5.8in) notebook to finish.

YOU WILL NEED

☐ Linen measuring 11x21in (28x53cm), and a square of muslin

☐ Embroidery floss – red, pink, brown and green

☐ A5 (8.3x5.8in) notebook

☐ General sewing supplies, including needle, scissors, pins, etc

Why not fill in the apple using long and short stitch (see page 40)?

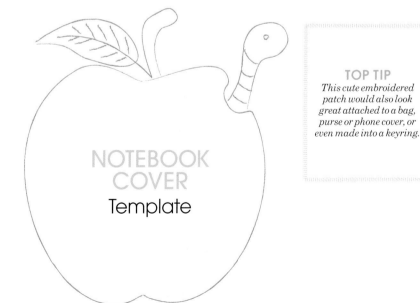

NOTEBOOK COVER
Template

TOP TIP
This cute embroidered patch would also look great attached to a bag, purse or phone cover, or even made into a keyring.

Use bias binding to cover all your seams and raw edges – and give a great finish at the same time!

Recreate the nostalgic memories of 1950s advertisements with these classic quilted kitchen appliance covers.

Do you remember those crisp pen-and-ink line drawing advertisements from the 1950s? Pick up a copy of any women's magazine from the decade and you're bound to find a woman with a huge smile on her face promoting the latest product. Susie's inspiration came from one of the very men responsible for creating those popular advertisements.

"It was my father!" she laughs. "He worked as an illustrator in the 1950s, drawing advertisements for our local newspaper, the *South Wales Evening Post*." This classic style is easy to convert into embroidery and just perfect for bringing a spot of nostalgia into your kitchen.

Uses just three stitches!

1 Cut out all your pieces of fabric before you start stitching. Make sure your appliance sizes match these listed below. If not, make adjustments, remembering to add a ½in (1cm) seam allowance.

2 The small cover measures 12½in (32cm) long, 8¾in (22cm) high and 6¼in (16cm) deep. This will fit an average two-slice toaster. Cut the following pieces in your main fabric, batting and lining:
• Two pieces 13½x9½in (34x24cm) for the front and back of the cover.
• Two pieces 9½x7in (24x18cm) for the sides of the cover.
• One piece 13½x7in (34x18cm) for the top of the cover.

3 The large cover measures 16¼in (41cm) long, 16in (35cm) high and 9½in (24cm) deep. This will fit a food processor or bread maker. For this version, cut the following pieces out of main fabric, batting and lining:
• Two pieces 17x14½in (43x37cm) for the front and back of the cover.
• Two pieces 14½x10¼in (37x26cm) for the sides of the cover.
• One piece 17x10¼in (43x26cm) for the top of the cover.

4 You are now ready to start on the embroidery. Your first job is to trace the motif onto one of the front pieces of fabric (you can do this two-thirds of the way along, as Susie has, or place it centrally if you prefer). Trace as accurately as you can, using our guide on page 18, because your stitches will need to cover the lines. Alternatively you could use a washable fabric pen.

bright
ideas!

this set would
make a great
wedding gift!

try tracing your
own designs
from ads in
**vintage
magazines**

*Keep your food processor
hidden under a stylishly
embroidered white cover.*

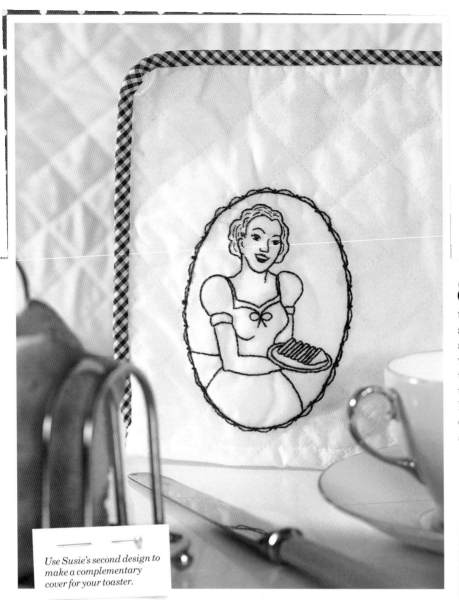

Use Susie's second design to make a complementary cover for your toaster.

8 Join the fabric pieces using a ½in (1cm) seam allowance and keeping the wrong sides together so that the seams are on the outside. Trim the seam allowance and cover the seams with bias tape. Start with the two seams that run across the top sides of the cover, then bind the sides and top with a single length of bias tape. The bias tape will cleverly hide the raw edges of the fabric as well as the batting.

5 Secure the fabric in an embroidery hoop and using two strands of embroidery floss, embroider over all the lines of the design in charcoal grey split stitch. If you want to make any of the lines bolder (for example, the oval outline) then you could use chain stitch instead of split stitch. You can use any charcoal or red embroidery floss you have in your thread stash – or why not change the colors to match your kitchen and your choice of bias binding?

6 When it comes to adding the fine details, such as the eyelashes, you may prefer to use one strand of embroidery floss. With the red thread, work French knots around the oval border and fill in the lips using satin stitch. Try using seed beads in place of the French knots in the border – these will have a great decorative effect, but be aware that you'll have to hand wash your covers instead.

7 Now apply the fusible batting to the reverse of each piece using a hot iron. You're now ready to quilt the cover, following the lines on the batting. If you use non-fusible batting, lay strips of masking tape to guide you instead. Make sure that you don't stitch over your embroidery – stop by the outer oval.

9 Make up the lining in the same way as the cover, except that you should have the seams on the wrong side. Slip the lining inside the cover. Turn under the bottom raw edges using a ½in (1cm) hem and stitch the cover and lining together.

Using just two colors means that this retro design still has a stylish, modern feel. Alternatively you could tweak the color scheme to match your kitchen!

Beautiful bed linen

designed by Jenny Cook

Brighten up some plain bed linen with these dainty pink roses, embroidered in a simple satin stitch.

Vary the colors of the flower petals if you'd like the stitching to coordinate with your existing bedroom décor.

D oes your bedroom need a breath of fresh air? Get out your needle and thread and decorate all your plain sheets and pillowcases with these delicate roses. You can complete each flower in just a few hours and all you need to learn is one simple stitch. Satin stitch is one of the most basic of all embroidery stitches and once you've mastered it, your bed linen will be covered in beautiful roses. Just check out our guide on page 38 for everything you need.

There are plenty of shops that sell classic white linen bedding, suitable for this type of embroidery. You could also try looking around your local antiques market. We recommend you use good quality bed linen so it will last you a lifetime. You'll also find it easier to stitch onto because they will be made of thicker fabric. Get stitching and soon you'll be having sweet dreams every night…

A great heirloom project

1 A single sheet will take about 14 large roses, leaving 8in (20cm) at either end for tucking under, but you can stitch as many or as few as you like.

2 To begin, trace the design on page 72 onto your sheet or pillowcase, using our guide on page 18. The whole design is worked in satin stitch using one strand of floss. Using an embroidery hoop, start stitching with the darkest green thread and work through to the pale pink. Follow the direction of the stitches as shown in the stitch guide on page 72.

3 Get the sheets and pillowcases ready for your bed by washing and pressing your stitching. Iron the back of your design gently with a towel underneath to avoid flattening your stitches.

TOP TIP
If you don't have time to stitch the bed linen, you could just embroider a rosebud onto cotton fabric and make it into a little drawstring bag. Or why not embroider one onto the corner of a table mat?

*Wake up and smell the roses
– they're even nicer when
you've stitched them yourself.*

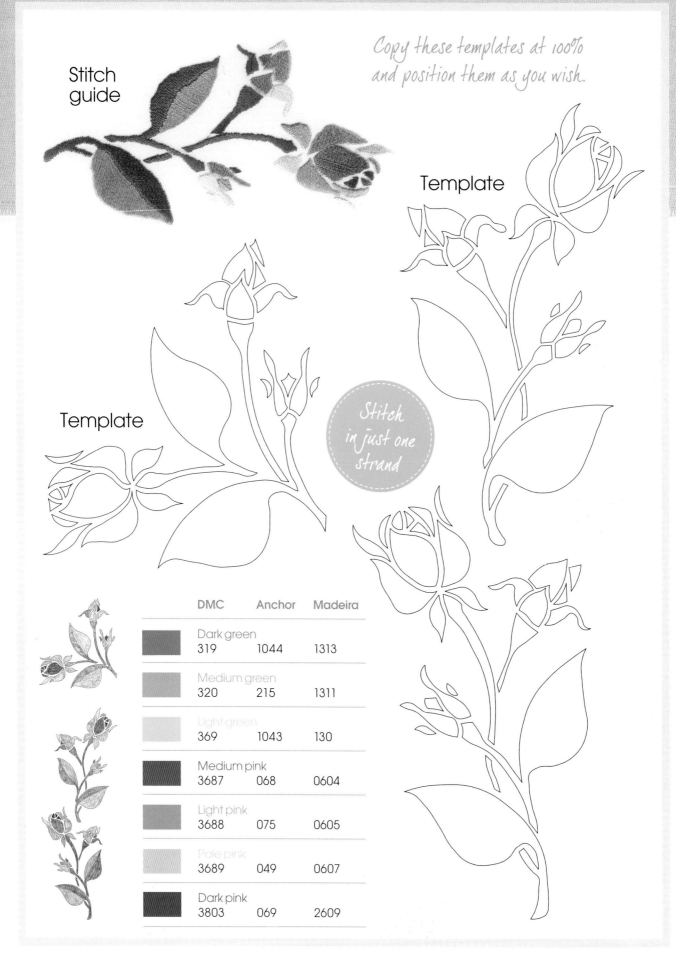

Stitch guide

Copy these templates at 100% and position them as you wish.

Template

Template

Stitch in just one strand

	DMC	Anchor	Madeira
Dark green	319	1044	1313
Medium green	320	215	1311
Light green	369	1043	130
Medium pink	3687	068	0604
Light pink	3688	075	0605
Pale pink	3689	049	0607
Dark pink	3803	069	2609

Twine heart sachet

designed by Rebecca Preston

Bring some rustic charm into your home with our simple sachet.

Perfect first couching project

1 Start by drawing a heart shape onto your fabric using pencil or a vanishing fabric pen.

2 Thread the twine onto a large crewel needle and begin with it on the reverse of the fabric. Pull it through at the bottom point of the heart, and lay it out along the outline.

3 Work your couching stitches in a single strand of coordinating thread, every few millimeters along the heart outline. Pull the twine back through to the reverse when you've finished. Then attach a button in the center of the heart.

4 Sew your fabric into a sachet, stuff it, and attach a hanging loop of twine at the top before you sew the final seam.

YOU WILL NEED

☐ Plain or patterned fabric

☐ Natural twine

☐ A large button

☐ General sewing supplies, including needles, scissors, pins, etc

For a bolder look, use contrasting fabric and thread shades.

Stuff your sachet with lavender, or rice mixed with aromatherapy oil.

Storage box

designed by Jenny Ellory

Turn your bedroom into a sanctuary and banish clutter with these gorgeous storage box ideas. This captivating fabric by hip designer Amy Butler provides a modern take on florals. We've coupled it with sequins, seed beads and buttons to create sophisticated results by using some surprisingly simple techniques.

YOU WILL NEED

☐ Bold floral fabric – check instructions for sizes

☐ Iron-on interfacing

☐ Wooden box

☐ Seed beads, pearl beads, sequins & buttons

☐ Grosgrain & sheer ribbons

☐ Notebook

Encourage teens to get crafty-and stay neat-by helping them make this pretty set

Antique chic

1 Cut a 9¾in (25cm) square of fabric to fit around the foam pad in the box.

2 Sew a pretty collection of buttons, seed and pearl beads and a ribbon bow to areas of the flower to decorate. Make sure to use matching colors, and a fine needle to go through the beads.

3 Wrap the finished fabric piece around the foam pad, neatly tucking the edges in, and secure with stitching or double-sided tape at the back.

Keep a note

1 Cut a piece of fabric to leave a ¾in (2cm) border around your book cover when laid flat. Use double-sided tape to secure the fabric down the spine, front and back.

2 Snip it at each end of the spine and tuck under. Fold the top and bottom around the cover, securing with tape inside. Next, fold the corners in, and then the sides.

3 Stick the notebook liner (the first page at the front and back) down over the fabric edges for a neater look. Thread a few beads onto ribbons and wrap them around to finish.

1 To make this easy bag, cut two pieces of fabric, both 12½x16½in (32x42cm). Pin them together with the right sides facing each other, and sew across the bottom and along the long sides, stopping 1¾in (4.5cm) from the top.

2 Next, fold over the the top of your fabric by 1¼in(3cm). Stitch about ¾in (1.5cm) down to make a tube. You can also stitch along the very top of the fold to finish the edge if you like.

3 Turn the bag the right way out and press with an iron to remove any creases. Thread ribbon or cord through the channel you created at the top, and tie together at the ends. Here's a tip: attach a safety pin to the end of your ribbon and use this to help you thread it through.

Baby suit

designed by Rebecca Preston

Give their little outfits a truly personal touch with this sweet strawberry.

1 Transfer the template below onto the central chest area of the bodysuit, following our guide on page 18. If you want to, you can iron interfacing onto the back, to add stability to the fabric.

2 Using the white floss, stitch the strawberry design. Use split stitch for the leaves, stem stitch for the main outline and lazy daisy stitches for the seeds. When you're finished, make sure you knot the thread firmly and neatly trim the ends, so nothing can catch.

So quick and simple!

If you use colored thread, make sure it's machine washable!

YOU WILL NEED

☐ Embroidery floss in white

☐ A plain red bodysuit

☐ Embroidery hoop

☐ Iron-on interfacing (optional)

☐ General sewing supplies, including needle, scissors, pins, etc

BABY SUIT
Template

Heart sachets

designed by Heather Kingley-Heath

Fill your stitching with love and make these pretty scented sachets. Feeling adventurous? Try your hand at tea dyeing your fabric first to produce some extra-special results

Don't you just love to open your closet and take out delicately perfumed clothes? So does Heather. "Every year, come lavender harvest time, I've said I'll make lavender bags," says Heather, "and I never have, until now, but my new cottage just has such a wonderful garden that I just had to."

Heather's delicately embroidered scented hearts seem to hark back to another era, with that slightly faded romantic look. "It's tea," reveals Heather. "I soak the fabric in tea and it gives this lovely effect, almost like the sepia tones in photographs. I had no idea that tea could be so versatile until I was doing my Textiles degree. I knew someone who used it as a wash on some of their art work but unfortunately, us poor students lived in some very damp, cold rooms. Just before our end of year show my friend

discovered that damp, cold tea wash makes all your work go horribly mouldy! At least you don't have to worry about that with tea dyeing."

Heather's hearts really are home-grown because not only did the lavender come out of her garden but she also makes her own potpourri. "I use lemon balm, rose petals and a variety of herbs – whatever's growing at the time. It's a very gentle scent but good for keeping the moths at bay."

As far as the embroidery is concerned, it's simple but effective. "I always use the same basic stitches, just in different ways with different thicknesses of thread," says Heather. "It means that the hearts are really very easy to make. And you can have a cup of tea when you've finished!"

Discover easy and quick finishes, using homemade cord and pretty buttons

Master the art of stitching perfect curves for really professional lettering

Heather's tea dyeing tips
A self-confessed tea dyeing addict for years, Heather has this advice for people just starting out. "Tea dyeing gives a mottled finish which will enhance the antique effect of your fabric. Try using different varieties of tea and it'll actually give you lots of different colors of fabric.

Ingredients for your sachet:
☐ Surface embroidery fabric –
two pieces 7x7in (18x18cm), pink

☐ Embroidery floss listed in the key

☐ Crewel embroidery needle – size 9

☐ Embroidery hoop

☐ Potpourri

☐ Sewing equipment including pins,
scissors and sewing cotton

Stitching your garden and lavender sachets

Here's everything you need to know
to get a professional finish

1 The first part of the job is to transfer
the design onto the fabric. If you need
to brush up on transfer methods, turn
to page 18.

2 The lovely thing about this design
is that you can work it in any order.
You also get a rather nice sense of
achievement completing each motif
before moving to the next.

3 Follow the illustration opposite for
the stitches and colors you need to
use for each part of the design. Thread
your needle with two strands unless
otherwise instructed.

4 If you are new to freestyle embroidery,
turn to page 24 for all the stitches
needed in this design. Some of the design
appears outside the dashed stitching
line for the heart so that it looks as if
the design continues round the heart.
When you have finished, press.

	Anchor	DMC	Madeira
Pink	27	893	0413
Mid purple	86	3608	0709
Pale green	253	472	1414
Pale yellow	292	3078	0102
Yellow	302	743	0113

Now try it in antique colors!

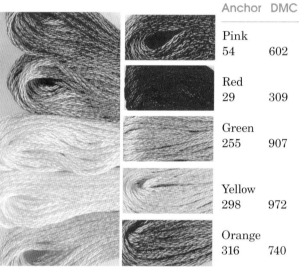

	Anchor	DMC	Madeira
Pink	54	602	0702
Red	29	309	0507
Green	255	907	1410
Yellow	298	972	0107
Orange	316	740	0203

Give your sachets an antique look by tea dyeing your fabric, then swap the colors shown in the key above for these more dramatic shades. It'll give your design added emphasis on the darker fabric.

More for you to enjoy

Tea dyed options

Tea dyeing your fabric before stitching is every bit as easy as it sounds. It's a process that you need to carry out before you start any embroidery.

First, make yourself a large cup of tea in a bowl (minus milk and sugar!). Brew until it's a reasonable color then immerse your fabric. Swish it around, remove it, wring it out and let the material dry naturally on your clothesline. Experiment with different types of tea to get different effects.

Lazy daisy stitch

Chain stitch

Chain stitch (in one strand)

Satin stitch

French knots

The embroidery text reads "Sweet lavender"

TURN YOUR STITCHING INTO A SACHET

1 Trim the heart to ½in(1cm) outside the dashed line – this ½in(1cm) forms your seam allowance.

2 Place back and front right sides together, pin and stitch. You will need to leave an opening between the two 'X's' marked on the pattern. Clip the curved edges towards the stitched line (taking care not to cut the stitching line). This gives your heart smooth curves.

3 Turn your heart out the right way and stuff with pot pourri. You can now slip stitch the opening closed.

4 You can now decorate the edge with blanket stitch if you like. Finish by adding a loop and button at the top and a plump tassel at the bottom.

FINISHING TOUCH

An easy tassel to give your sachet a professional finish.

1 You need to cut a piece of card slightly longer than the length you want your tassel to be. Wrap embroidery floss around the card to the thickness you would like your tassel – plump tassels always look good.

Anchor	DMC	Madeira
Use two strands of embroidery floss		
Pale blue		
117	341	0901
Mid blue		
176	793	0906
Green		
254	472	1414
Pale lavender		
342	211	0801
Sea green		
875	3817	1702

Now try it in antique colors!

Anchor	DMC	Madeira
Dark blue		
177	792	0905
Purple		
1030	3746	0804
Light green		
279	734	1610
Orange		
328	3341	0303
Dark sea green		
876	3816	1202

You can stitch the sweet lavender design on antique-dyed fabric too (turn to page 81 for instructions). Swap the shades in the main key for those in this box to make your design look much bolder on the fabric.

2 Cut a length of floss and thread a needle. Take the needle under the wrapped thread and tie a knot at one end, making sure that it is nice and tight. Now you can cut through the bundle of threads at the opposite end.

3 Work a wrapping thread around the head of the tassel about ¼in (5mm) from the top, then thread the ends back down the body of the tassel. Finish by teasing out the individual strands.

Hair clips

designed by Anchor

Simple running
stitch and vibrant
backstitch are
used to great effect
on these cute clips.

1 Use the templates below to cut felt
pieces of each shape. Place pieces a
and b together and embroider the edges
together with blanket stitch, to make a
pocket that the clip will fit inside. Use
embroidery floss in the color of your
choice and work with three strands.

2 Take template pieces c and d. Work
the blanket stitch around piece c
(using embroidery floss in the color of
your choice). Embroider a small star
on piece d and then embellish it with
French knots.

3 Use running stitches in shade 332
to attach piece d on top of piece c.
Finally, glue the circles to piece a. Slide
the hair clip into the felt pocket to finish.

YOU WILL NEED

☐ Anchor embroidery floss,
1 skein each of colors:
1, 13, 54, 98, 187, 240 and 332

☐ Felt in various colors

☐ Hair clips

☐ General sewing supplies,
including scissors, pencil,
craft glue, etc.

Ideal for little girls!

If you need to, adjust the shape of felt pieces a and b to match the size of your clips.

HAIR CLIPS Templates

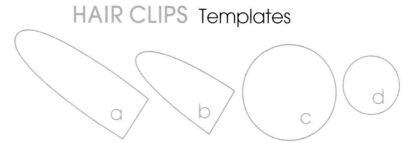

a

b

c

d

Machine embroidery basics

Embroidering with your sewing machine is the on-trend way to give your home the handmade touch. Here's your guide to the basics…

Using a sewing machine

Get all the know-how on using your sewing machine, so you can create fabulous machine embroidery projects!

Whether you're a stitching novice or just need a refresher, here's our guide to finding your way around a sewing machine. Every machine varies slightly, so some of these functions might work differently, or yours might have extra features. Refer to your manual for exactly how to use your machine.

THREAD FEED

Your spool of thread sits at the top of the machine. It threads through a series of numbered channels and loops before it reaches the needle. This maintains an even thread tension and avoids tangles. Your machine will have a numbered dial that can be raised or lowered to adjust the tension as your fabric requires.

NEEDLE

A sewing machine needle moves in and out of the fabric without going all the way through, as in hand sewing. Most machines come with a needle in place, but your manual will explain how to change it. Standard needles are typically size 11 or 12. For tougher jobs, such as sewing denim or very heavy curtains, go for a larger number – 18 or 19. When sewing a fine fabric such as organza or sheer net, use a fine size 8. When you buy your fabric, it's worth asking which needle is best for the job.

FOOT

This is the metal attachment that sits beneath your needle and holds your fabric in place. There's a lever to move it up and down. Raise it up when positioning your fabric and move it down when sewing. The foot works with the feed dogs underneath the fabric to hold it in place. Your machine should come with a basic presser foot, but there are dozens of speciality feet, including a darning foot for machine embroidery.

BOBBIN

This small plastic or metal spool sits in a special housing under the sewing area, below the foot and needle. Check your manual for exactly how to load your bobbin. Once loaded, the bobbin thread and top thread feeds meet to form each stitch.

STITCH SELECTOR

Dials, switches, knobs…the method used to change the stitch type varies between machines, but the principle is the same. You'll mostly use the basic straight stitch and zigzag, but once you're more confident, try some of the more decorative stitches your machine has to offer.

HAND WHEEL

Use the hand wheel to move the needle up and down manually, to control the sewing line in tight spots and corners. To avoid getting tangled threads, always turn the wheel toward you. To wind bobbins, you'll need to disengage the needle action by pulling out this wheel or pressing a switch. Check your manual for how to do this on your machine.

STITCH WIDTH

Sometimes this function is built in, so the machine automatically adjusts this as you change the stitch type. If your machine has a width dial, leave it at 0 for straight stitches because the needle doesn't need to move from side to side. For other stitches, simply adjust the width as needed, practising on a scrap of fabric first.

STITCH LENGTH

A dial or knob will enable you to change the length of your stitches, whether they're simple straight stitches, zig-zags or any other pattern. A long stitch length is useful for creating quick tacking lines. For regular stitching, aim for a length of around 2 or 2.5, but experiment with the stitch length and practice on a fabric scrap.

REVERSE STITCHING

Most machines have a button or switch to enable you to sew in the reverse direction. Even older machines should have a method for reverse stitching – it's handy for embroidering various shapes. Stitching forwards and backwards for a few centimetres will also secure your threads at the start and end of your stitching.

FOOT PEDAL

The foot pedal is connected to the machine and sits on the floor. The pedal is pressure-sensitive, so gentle pressure results in slow stitching, while pressing harder will run the motor faster. Some machines also have a separate speed control, which gives you even more command over your pace.

Machine embroidery

Learn how to use your sewing machine to create quick but gorgeous embroidery projects with an ultra-modern feel…

While hand embroidery can be wonderfully relaxing, using your sewing machine to embroider is becoming hugely popular and creative. Freehand machine embroidery involves using your sewing machine in a 'freehand' style rather than working in straight lines, so you have more freedom to 'doodle' with your machine and work the stitches in any direction. The freehand style turns your sewing machine into an artistic tool that you can use to create designs on fabric, often combining it with appliqué motifs.

To do machine embroidery, you don't need much special equipment. Aside from fabric and spools of thread, you'll need to have a sewing machine that allows you to lower the feed dogs. The feed dogs are like metal teeth in the plate of the sewing machine that hold onto your fabric and evenly move it, or feed it, past the needle. Lowering the feed dogs enables your fabric to move freely as you stitch. You'll also need to use an embroidery hoop to keep the fabric taut, and a darning or free-motion foot to attach to your sewing machine, to keep the fabric smooth.

Purchase a darning foot at your local sewing shop. Consult your sewing machine manual for instructions on how to attach your darning foot, because all machines are different.

Mount your fabric into an embroidery hoop, but in the opposite way to normal, so the inner ring is facing up. On your machine, drop the feed dogs and thread the needle. Lift up your darning foot and place your hoop underneath.

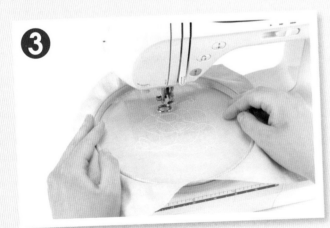

Hold the hoop firmly with both hands. Begin sewing, moving the hoop in any direction. Use a piece of scrap fabric to practice making squiggles and shapes. It takes a while to get the hang of it, so don't get discouraged.

Once you feel a bit more confident, try stitching some shapes, starting with squares. Then move on to circles, and finally hearts. Practice making double outlines, which creates a wonderful sketchy look.

Appliqué motifs

Add another dimension with appliqué motifs – here's how to use fusible webbing to attach them and interfacing to strengthen them…

When you're using appliqué motifs as part of your machine embroidery design, it's best to pin them in place on the background fabric before sewing them on. For very small pieces, you could use fabric glue instead of pins – just take care not too use too much, or things will get messy. Alternatively, you could tack the motifs in place and remove the thread later.

Another option is to use fusible webbing. Fusible webbing is a paper-backed heat-sensitive film that you iron onto the wrong side of the appliqué fabric. You then draw the shape of the motif, cut it out and remove the paper backing. Then iron your motif in place onto your background fabric. Most fusible webbing is only temporary so you'll need to stitch around or over your appliqué motif to secure it.

If your appliqué fabric or background fabric is a bit thin or flimsy, you can stiffen it and give it extra strength by backing it with interfacing. Interfacing is available as sew-in or fusible types, which means that you iron it on. Fusible interfacing has a shiny, bumpy side and a smooth side. The shiny, bumpy side has adhesive on it – this is the side that needs to be placed on the wrong side of your fabric, and then ironed in place. Take care not to let the interfacing pucker the fabric, because it will be very difficult to remove it afterwards without ruining the fabric.

HOW TO... USE FUSIBLE WEBBING
A hassle-free trick that will be handy to have in your workbox.

Fusible webbing is a thin layer of adhesive attached to a paper backing. Trace your template onto the smooth, paper side.

Roughly cut around your chosen shape. Place the shape paper side up onto the reverse of your fabric. Now iron over the top to set the adhesive on the fabric.

Cut out your shape from the fabric and remove the paper backing. Place your shape adhesive side down on the background fabric, making sure it's in the right place.

Iron over the top to set it in place – protect delicate fabrics by placing a cloth between the fabric and the iron. Now you're ready to stitch, by hand or machine.

Darning foot
A darning foot differs from a normal presser foot, because it allows you to stitch in whatever direction you like while still keeping your fabric smooth. Each make varies, so check the instructions for how to attach it. Once fitted, slide the fabric under the foot, drop the needle and you're ready to start! Most darning feet can be moved up and down, allowing room for a hoop underneath.

A darning foot is vital for machine embroidery.

Combine different fabrics for a textured look. Linens fray quite a bit, cottons fray a little and felts don't fray at all.

Machine stitches

Learn how to use your sewing machine to work all sorts of machine embroidery stitches, techniques and styles...

Getting started

Start off by doodling and playing with the different stitches on your sewing machine. Play with straight stitches, in different lengths and colors, then move on to zigzag stitches in different sizes and types. Then try making scribbles and loops. Just have fun!

Make shapes

Move on to making basic outlines for various shapes, such as circles, squares, hearts and flowers. Practice making double outlines by going around the shape again – your aim should be to get the shapes tidy but still sketchy.

Start shading

Once you're confident making outlines, try coloring them in, which is called shading. Move the fabric backwards and forwards to fill the outline with stitches of thread, a bit like satin stitch in hand embroidery.

Appliqué motifs

Add an extra dimension to your shapes with appliqué. Cut out shaped pieces of fabric and attach with straight stitch or zigzag stitch outlines, or try stitching over both the appliqué shape and the background fabric.

Make sure your background and appliqué fabrics work together, then play with different stitch styles to find the best way to attach them.

Layered appliqué

Put together all the skills you've practiced and you can create gorgeous designs like this present – it's layered up with appliqué motifs, outlining, shading and other interesting stitch styles.

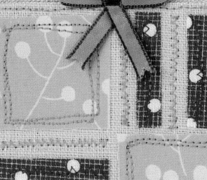

Freehand machine embroidery

PIER EMBROIDERED CUSHION *from Lara Sparks, www.rume.co.uk*

CHRISTMAS PUDDING DECORATION
www.fromthewilde.com

CREW NECK APPLIQUÉ BEAR T-SHIRT
www.marksandspencer.com

lthough freehand machine embroidery has been an up-and-coming craft for some time, it's exploded in popularity recently. As a fairly young craft, it has a distinctly modern look and its potential is only limited by your own imagination!

Machine embroidery will give you a completely different (but equally wonderful) style of stitching to hand embroidery. You don't have to carefully work each stitch by hand, so you can be a lot more free and creative with where and how you let the stitches run over the fabric.

Freestyle machine embroidery doesn't require a special or expensive sewing machine – just a standard model that can produce straight and zigzag stitches is fine. As long as you can drop the feed dogs on your machine (those thin metal bars with teeth under the needle), you'll be able to freely move the fabric around in any direction you wish. You can also experiment: try using different colored threads in the top and

the bobbin to create interesting effects, and you could vary the tension to create looser stitches with both threads showing.

With just a little bit of practice on your sewing machine, you can create all sorts of gorgeous projects, from luggage tags to embellished clothing. It's also super-easy to combine machine embroidery with appliqué, layering fabrics to create pretty designs and blocks of colors. Be inspired by some of these gorgeous machine embroidery items from the high street…

CHRISTMAS AT… PERSONALIZED STAG CUSHION
www.fromthewilde.com

CAT HEART T-SHIRT
(FAR RIGHT)
www.mandco.com

Machine

embroidery projects

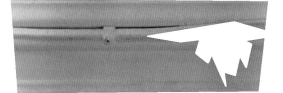

Luggage tag

designed by *Rebecca Preston*

Wherever you travel, you'll be able to spot your suitcase with this unique stitched tag.

1 To make a sturdy luggage tag, sandwich the raw ends of a ribbon loop between two pieces of felt. Use your sewing machine to stitch all the way around using a straight running stitch.

2 Cut out simple circles in different sizes from a variety of patterned fabrics – choose contrasting colors to create a textured look. Then use a contrasting thread to finish the look – here, we've used white to pick out the white polka dots.

3 Stitch each circle into place with freehand machine embroidery, starting with the largest circle and layering the circles. Your stitched circles look best if they don't exactly follow the outlines of the fabric, in a sketchy style.

YOU WILL NEED

- ☐ Two pieces of colored felt, both approx 2½x4in (6x10 cm)

- ☐ Scraps of fabric in coordinating colors

- ☐ Ribbon, 1x12in (2.5x30cm)

- ☐ General sewing supplies, including scissors, pins, etc

Great for a stylish gift!

Heart set

designed by Rebecca Preston

This cute card is so simple to make with its layered fabrics and stylish sketchy stitching.

PRETTY CARD

1 To make our quick appliqué card, cut out a small felt heart using the template opposite. Cut a square of felt that's larger than the heart, and then another square of patterned fabric that's larger than the felt square. Don't worry about cutting perfect square shapes by hand – with freehand embroidery, the appliqué layers often look better with a few imperfections.

2 Use iron-on fusible webbing to attach the heart shape to the felt square, then attach this to the patterned square.

3 Using your sewing machine, freehand embroider outlines around the heart and both of the squares. Your outlines don't need to be neat – a sketchy double outline looks great. Finish off by gluing your fabric layers to the front of your blank card.

YOU WILL NEED

☐ Colored felt and coordinating patterned fabric

☐ A blank white card

☐ General sewing supplies, including scissors, pins, etc

Great for your first project!

Experiment with different color schemes to suit a special occasion or person.

These designs would also look great as brooches – why not make some as a gift?

Cute felt buttons are great as handmade gifts, and add a touch of fun to any outfit.

COVERED BUTTONS

1 Decide which style of button you want to make – a simple self-covered button (on the right in the photo) or an appliqué button (shown on the left).

2 For the simple self-covered button, cut a piece of felt large enough to wrap around the button. Freehand embroider a heart outline onto it in a coordinating color. Attach the fabric to the self-cover buttons following the instructions that accompany the pack.

3 To make the appliqué button, cut a heart shape out of felt and cut a piece of patterned fabric large enough to wrap around the button. Attach the heart shape to the fabric and machine embroider a heart outline around the outside edge. Attach the fabric to the self-cover buttons following the manufacturer's instructions.

These soft and simple felt buttons are super-stylish and great for beginners.

CARD & BUTTONS
Heart template

Trace our simple heart shape to create your own embroidered masterpieces!

YOU WILL NEED

☐ Self-cover buttons in 1in (29mm) and 1½in (38mm)

☐ Colored felt and coordinating patterned fabric

☐ General sewing supplies, including scissors, pins, etc

Heart cushion

designed by Rebecca Preston

YOU WILL NEED

- ☐ Four squares of cotton and linen fabrics, each measuring 8x8in (20x20cm), in coordinating colors and patterns

- ☐ Four squares of the same fabrics as above, each measuring 5x5in (12x12cm)

- ☐ One piece of backing fabric, measuring 15x15in (38x38cm)

- ☐ A coordinating button

- ☐ Sewing machine

- ☐ Embroidery hoop

- ☐ Cushion stuffing, such as small (non-spiky) feathers, polyester hollowfiber filling, or even scraps of old fabrics

- ☐ Iron-on fusible webbing

- ☐ General sewing supplies, including scissors, pins, fabric marker, etc

Spread the love with this irresistible patchwork cushion, decorated with gorgeous machine embroidery.

Patchwork is so on-trend at the moment, and once you've mastered outlining in freehand machine embroidery, you'll be able to whip up a cushion like this in an hour or two! It's contemporary yet full of retro charm, with cute appliqué hearts in different patterned fabrics – it will look great on any sofa or comfy chair.

We combined linen and cotton fabrics in gorgeous blues and polka dots, then used bright turquoise thread to tie it all together. We've provided the heart template on the opposite page, but you could experiment with your own motif design, such as stars, butterflies or apples. If you like, you could change the colors completely to match the color theme in your living room. Get creative and see what happens!

Practice sketchy outlines

1 Trace the heart template (right) onto a piece of fusible webbing using a pencil and drawing on the smooth side. Roughly cut around the shape, iron it onto the back of one of your 4¾x4¾in (12x12cm) fabric squares, and cut it out. Repeat this for the remaining three hearts on the other fabrics.

2 Cut out four squares of different fabrics, measuring 8x8in (20x20cm) each. Lay out all your fabric hearts and squares, mixing and matching the colors until you're happy with the final look. Fuse a heart to the center of each square using an iron.

TOP TIP

If you'd rather create your own templates, make sure you choose simple shapes – birds, flowers and stars would all work well.

A large pearlized button is
the perfect finishing touch
to this retro chic cushion.

3 Freehand machine embroider a
double outline in a contrasting
thread shade around each heart shape.
With the right sides facing, sew two of
your patches together using a ½in (1cm)
seam allowance. Repeat with the other
two. Open and press the seams flat.

4 With right sides facing, sew your two
sets together, lining up the seams
at the middle. Stitch a button over the
central seam at the front. With right sides
facing, sew your front patchwork piece
and your backing fabric together, leaving
a 4in (10cm) turning gap. Turn and fill
with stuffing. Slip stitch the gap closed.

*Your gorgeous cushion makes
a fantastic gift that will
warm any heart this winter!*

HEART
Template

Heart cardigan

designed by Rebecca Preston

Add a personal touch to your clothes by stitching handmade motifs onto plain areas.

Create your own fashion items!

1 Choose the item of clothing you want to embellish, and plan where to stitch the heart. We've provided a template below, so enlarge or reduce it on a photocopier as needed. Trace your heart shape onto a scrap of fabric and cut it out.

2 Use a sewing machine to freehand embroider the heart shape onto a scrap of patterned fabric – make sure this square is slightly larger than the finished square you want.

3 Back this square with iron-on fusible webbing and then attach it to your item of clothing using an iron. Outline the square with freehand embroidery, directly through the clothing. Trim any excess fabric around the square.

CARDIGAN
Heart template

YOU WILL NEED

☐ An item of clothing to embellish

☐ Scraps of coordinating fabric

☐ General sewing supplies, including scissors, pins, etc

Use a sewing machine to freehand embroider the heart shape.

Tea towel

designed by Abigail Barker

YOU WILL NEED

☐ Fabric, approx 15¾x25½in (40x65cm)

☐ Embroidery floss in your choice of colors

☐ Embroidery stabilizer (optional, for thinner fabric)

☐ Water-erasable fabric pen

☐ Embroidery hoop

☐ General sewing supplies, including scissors, pins, etc

TOP TIP
Use a medium-weight fabric, either 100% cotton, 100% linen, or a mix of the two. Cotton is less expensive but linen can be used to dry delicate plates and silverware without scratching.

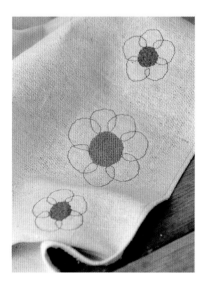

Brighten up your kitchen with colorful embroidered motifs – these flowers are full of sunshine!

Whether it's as a personalized gift or a special accessory for your own kitchen, our simple machine-embroidered tea towel is a great way to add a splash of color to your washing up! The simple flower shapes make this an ideal first project for anyone new to machine embroidery. Practice on a spare piece of fabric first and you'll soon get the hang of making these flowers – you could even stitch them onto other accessories in your kitchen!

Great project for beginners

1 Using the templates on the next page and a water-erasable fabric pen, draw your three flowers onto the fabric at the shorter end – we placed our flowers approximately 2½in (6cm) from the raw edge of the fabric.

2 If your fabric is quite thin, back it with an embroidery stabilizer – this avoids the fabric puckering and helps with densely stitched areas.

3 Mount the fabric in a hoop, gently pulling the opposite sides to create a firm, tight tension, and tightening the hoop as you go.

4 Make sure you lower the feed dogs on your sewing machine and attach your darning foot. Use the same color of thread in the top thread and the bobbin thread. Select a running stitch (you can choose the stitch length) and an even tension, testing the stitches on a scrap of the same fabric if necessary.

5 Starting with the larger middle flower, sew the center circle outline. Then fill in the center by moving the hoop back and forth. Do not over-work the same area. We worked in circular rows from the outside in and then added a 'looser' stitch coverage over the top. Finish the flower by sewing the petal outlines in a single line, in a smooth, continuous movement.

6 Repeat the above steps to machine embroider the two smaller flowers, repositioning the fabric in the hoop to ensure that your working area is in the center of the hoop.

7 Rinse the fabric in water to wash away the pen marks. Remove your embroidery stabilizer by cutting or tearing it away, following the manufacturer's instructions.

8 Hem the raw edges of the fabric to finish the tea towel.

*Choose shades of thread to match the colors in
your kitchen or your crockery.*

TEA TOWEL
Flower templates

Love Patchwork
978-1-57421-446-8
DO5414 **$19.99**

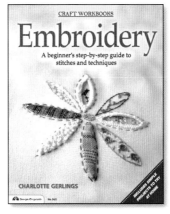

Embroidery
978-1-57421-500-7
DO5421 **$9.99**

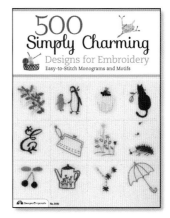

500 Simply Charming Designs for Embroidery
978-1-57421-509-0
DO5430 **$14.99**

Ultimate Cross Stitch Projects
978-1-57421-444-4
DO5415 **$19.99**

Cross Stitched Cards for the Holidays
978-1-57421-380-5
DO3503 **$9.99**

Sewing Pretty Little Things
978-1-57421-611-0
DO5301 **$19.99**

Sew Me! Sewing Basics
978-1-57421-423-9
DO5394 **$19.99**

Sew Me! Sewing Home Décor
978-1-57421-504-5
DO5425 **$14.99**

Soft Toys
978-1-57421-501-4
DO5422 **$9.99**

**Cross Stitched Cards for
Special Occasions**
978-1-57421-376-8
DO3500 **$9.99**

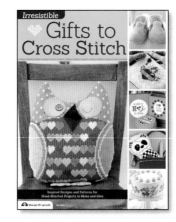

Irresistible Gifts to Cross Stitch
978-1-57421-445-1
DO5416 **$19.99**

Handmade for Christmas
978-1-57421-508-3
DO5429 **$14.99**

Lace Collection for Knitting
978-1-57421-447-5
DO5418 **$17.99**

Hip Knitting
978-1-57421-426-0
DO5397 **$12.99**

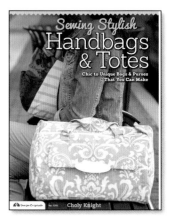

**Sewing Stylish
Handbags & Totes**
978-1-57421-422-2
DO5393 **$22.99**

Sew Baby
978-1-57421-421-5
DO5392 **$19.99**

Quilting & Applique
978-1-57421-502-1
DO5423 **$9.99**

**Making Jewelry with
T-Shirt Yarn**
978-1-57421-374-4
DO3498 **$8.99**